Passport's I

SOUTH AFRICA

FROM
THOMAS
COOK

PASSPORT BOOKS
a division of *NTC Publishing Group*
Lincolnwood, Illinois USA

Published by Passport Books,
a division of NTC Publishing Group,
4255 W. Touhy Avenue,
Lincolnwood (Chicago), Illinois
60646–1975 U.S.A.

Written by Paul Duncan

Original photography by Paul Kenward

Edited, designed, and produced by AA Publishing.
© The Automobile Association 1996.
Maps © The Automobile Association 1996.

Reprinted 1997

Library of Congress Catalog Card Number:
95-70289

ISBN 0-8442-9124-2

The contents of this publication are believed correct at the time of
printing. Nevertheless the publishers cannot accept responsibility for any
errors or omissions, for changes in the details given in this guide, or for
the consequences of any reliance on the information provided by the
same. Assessments of attractions, hotels, restaurants, and so forth are
based upon the author's own experience and therefore descriptions given
in this guide necessarily contain an element of subjective opinion that
may not reflect the publisher's opinion or dictate a reader's own
experiences on another occasion.
We have tried to ensure accuracy in this guide, but things do
change and we would be grateful if readers would advise us of any
inaccuracies they may encounter.

Published by AA Publishing (a trading name of Automobile Association
Developments Limited, whose registered office is Norfolk House,
Priestley Road, Basingstoke, Hampshire RG24 9NY. Registered number
1878835) and the Thomas Cook Group Ltd.

Published by Passport Books in conjunction with AA Publishing and the
Thomas Cook Group Ltd.

Color separation: BTB Colour Reproduction, Whitchurch, Hampshire,
England.

Printed by: Edicoes ASA, Oporto, Portugal.

Contents

About this Book

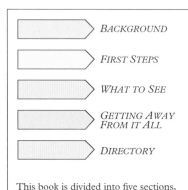

BACKGROUND

FIRST STEPS

WHAT TO SEE

GETTING AWAY
FROM IT ALL

DIRECTORY

This book is divided into five sections,
identified by the following colour coding

Beach huts at Muizenberg on the Cape
Peninsula, a popular resort since Victorian times

The **Background** gives an introduction
to the country – its history, geography,
politics, culture.

First Steps offers practical advice on
arriving and getting around.

What to See is an alphabetical listing of
places to visit, divided into four regions,
interspersed with tours.

Getting Away From it All highlights
places off the beaten track where it's
possible to relax and enjoy peace and
quiet.

Finally the **Directory** provides practical
information – from shopping and
entertainment to children and sport,
including a section on business matters.
Special highly illustrated features on
specific aspects of the country appear
throughout the book.

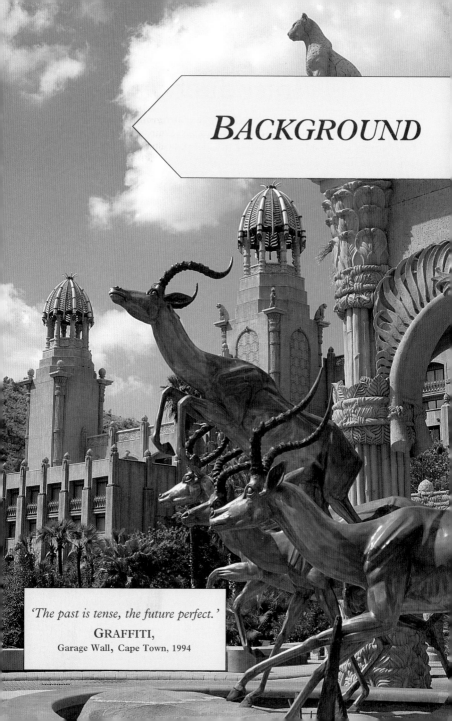

BACKGROUND

'The past is tense, the future perfect.'
GRAFFITI,
Garage Wall, Cape Town, 1994

Introduction

Now is a good time to go to South Africa. It is a beautiful country whose vast potential has remained undiscovered as a result of the policy of entrenched apartheid which sought to segregate black from white. Vilified by the international community, South Africa was marginalised. Things have now changed dramatically. In 1994 the African National Congress won the country's first democratic elections, bringing 350 years of white domination to a close. The image of millions queuing patiently in the African dawn to bury apartheid at the polling booths sent a wave of hope through the world that reason and reconciliation can triumph over hatred.

COUNTRY LOCATOR

Before the first millennium AD, the country south of the Limpopo River had long been inhabited only by nomadic hunter-gatherers using Stone Age tools and living in harmony with the environment. From the first millenium AD onwards, the ancestors of most of South Africa's black population were migrating into the country from further north. As these people spread out south and towards the coastal plains, they adapted the environment to their needs as pastoralists and farmers.

This process accelerated with the arrival of the white man who claimed the best land and set about destroying and enslaving its earlier inhabitants. Alienation of the land went hand in hand with loss of political independence, and the old cultures gradually diminished so that today only a fraction of the indigenous economic, religious and social customs, all of them inextricably interlinked, have survived.

Nevertheless, this is a rich country, sub-Saharan Africa's most sophisticated, with an important emerging art market and unique architecture. After centuries of immigration it has enormous cultural diversity, and its wildlife, landscape and natural treasures are second to none. In spite of all its problems of poverty, violence and an uncertain future, South Africa is one of the most enticing holiday destinations in the African continent.

> **MAPPING**
> The maps in this book use the following international country symbols:
>
> | | |
> |---|---|
> | LS Lesotho | MZ Mozambique |
> | NAM Namibia | RB Botswana |
> | SD Swaziland | ZW Zimbabwe |

Surveying the scene from Table Mountain's lofty viewing platform, reached by cable-car

SOUTH AFRICA

ZW
Messina
RB
Thohoyandou
Polokwane
MZ
Warmbad
Rustenburg
PRETORIA
Nelspruit
NAM
Mmabatho
JOHANNESBURG
Limpopo
Molopo
Klerksdorp
Ermelo
SD
Vryburg
Kroonstad
Upington
Welkom
Bethlehem
Vryheid
Kimberley
Pietermaritzburg
Kenhardt
Bloemfontein
LS
DURBAN
Springbok
Orange
De
Aar
Kokstad
Calvinia
Carnarvon
Port Shepstone
Beaufort
West
Cradock
Umtata
Graaff
Reinet
East London
Uitenhage
Grahamstown
Paarl
Worcester
George
Port Elizabeth
CAPE TOWN
Cape of
Good Hope
Mossel
Bay
Cape
Agulhas

0   100   200   300 km
0   100   200 miles

History

100,000BC
Human bones of this age from Swaziland show southern Africa already inhabited by *Homo sapiens.*

AD1–1500
Iron-working spreads through central and southern Africa, enabling Bantu people to move southwards and dominate the San and Khoikhoi peoples.

1488
Bartholomieu Dias rounds the Cape and reaches Mossel Bay.

1497
Vasco da Gama rounds the Cape and charts the sea route to India.

1652
Arrival of Jan van Riebeeck, first

AFRICAN PEOPLE

Apart from the San (Bushmen) and the Khoikhoi (Hottentots), about 90 per cent of southern Africa's total population are blacks whose ancestors migrated from the north. Some of these peoples dispersed into ever more groups; the Nguni tribes (including Swazi, Xhosa and Zulu) eventually settled along the eastern seaboard, while the Sotho groups (Basotho, Pedi and Tswana) inhabited the South African plateau. Others, such as the Zulus, went on to form themselves into strong kingdoms. Further elements of the black population are the descendants of West African slaves imported by white settlers, and migrant workers from neighbouring countries who, throughout this century, have crossed South Africa's borders to man the gold and diamond mines.

---

commander of the Dutch East India Company's Cape settlement.

1688
French Huguenots arrive.

1779
First of nine settler-Xhosa frontier wars in the Eastern Cape.

1795
First British occupation of the Cape.

1806
Second British occupation of the Cape.

1820
British settlers arrive in the Grahamstown area.

mid-1830s
The Great Trek into the interior as Boers grow resentful of British rule in the Cape colony.

1838
Battle of Blood River: a small force of Voortrekkers defeats the Zulu.

1850s
Independent Boer republics of Orange Free State and Transvaal are established.

1867
Discovery of the Hope diamond; the diamond rush begins.

1879
Battles of Isandhlwana and Rorke's Drift.

1880
First Anglo-Boer War (won by the Boers).

1886
Gold discovered. Johannesburg founded.

1899–1902
Second Anglo-Boer War (won by the British).

1910
Union of South Africa.

1923
Land Act makes it illegal for Africans to buy or lease land from Europeans outside

the reserves. Leads to formation of the African National Congress.

1927
Immorality Act bans sex outside marriage between the races (extended in 1950 making all sexual relations between white and other races illegal).

1948
Victory for the National Party in white elections.

1950
Suppression of Communism Act: practically any person or organisation hostile to government policy could be defined as Communist and banned, with no right of appeal. Repealed in 1990. Also Group Areas Act: non-whites moved to townships. Repealed in 1991.

Settlers' Monument, Grahamstown

A DUTCH COLONY
The settlement of the Cape by the Dutch in 1652 led to the occupation of much of southern Africa by Europeans. Settler numbers increased slowly; the majority were Dutch, but there were also Germans and French Huguenots. As the settlement expanded, borders were extended by farmers searching for more land. This culminated in conflict with the Xhosa on the eastern frontier (1779). In 1795 the British took over to prevent the colony falling into the hands of the French, but in 1803 handed it back. Following the Napoleonic wars they returned (1806), and in 1814 the colony ceded formally to the British Crown.

THE ZULU
Zulu history is dominated by the military genius of the famous Shaka, who became Zulu chief in 1816. He extended his power until most of the north was under his dominion, an era of terror that caused a ripple effect – the *Mfecane* – which led to fleeing clans colliding with settled peoples dotted across a wide area from Swaziland to Lesotho. It ended with Shaka's assassination by his half-brother, Dingane. Having neither Shaka's strength nor genius, Dingane is held responsible for the gradual erosion of Zulu rule in the traditional tribal homelands. In 1879 Britain annexed Zululand and imprisoned the Zulu king, Cetshwayo. Today, King Goodwill Zwelithini is titular head of the Zulu nation, while the 'traditional prime minister' is his uncle, Chief Mangosuthu Buthelezi.

THE GREAT TREK

In 1835, two groups of Dutch-speaking Boers quit the Cape for the unknown interior in the Great Trek. They felt that the colonial government had failed to provide protection against the Xhosa in the never-ending battle for land, while the abolition of slavery had robbed them of valued possessions. One group of Voortrekkers, led by Piet Retief, went into Zulu Natal where Dingane massacred their advance party. Revenge was the horrible battle of Blood River, followed by the establishment of the Republic of Natalia (1838) which Britain annexed. The Boers then trekked north and in 1860 founded the South African Republic (ZAR).

The other party of Voortrekkers trekked beyond the Vaal and Orange Rivers and proclaimed the Orange Free State (1854).

1952
Pass Laws: all black people over the age of 16 are required to carry a passbook. Repealed in 1986.

1953
Separate Amenities Act. Provided for separate amenities for white and non-white races. Repealed in 1990.

1958
Dr Hendrik Verwoerd becomes prime minister. Apartheid strictly enforced.

1960
Referendum for South African independence. Sharpeville Massacre: demonstrators against the Pass Laws are fired on (69 killed, 180 injured). Demonstration leads to banning of ANC.

1961
Birth of the Republic of South Africa.

1964
Rivonia Treason Trial: Nelson Mandela and seven other ANC members are sentenced to life imprisonment. South Africa excluded from Olympic Games.

1966
Verwoerd assassinated.

1970
Bantu Homelands Act: all black South Africans to become citizens of the tribal homelands, making them aliens in South Africa. Repealed in 1994.

1975
South Africa invades Angola.
1976
Black schoolchildren in Soweto reject enforced teaching of Afrikaans. Student riots lead to hundreds of deaths. **1977** Mandatory UN arms embargo. Steve Biko dies in detention.
1984
A new constitution allows three separate houses in parliament – for whites, Coloureds and Indians.
1985
ANC president Oliver Tambo, Rev Jesse Jackson, and Archbishop Huddleston head a 100,000-strong march through London demanding sanctions. State of emergency declared in sections of the country. Formation of the Congress of South African Trade Unions
1986
All Commonwealth leaders except Britain bar links with South Africa and cut imports.
1989
F W de Klerk becomes president.

1990
Mandela released. The ANC and other banned political organisations are legalised. National Party government abandons apartheid, and begins negotiations to end it. Southwest Africa gains independence from South Africa, becoming Namibia.
1992
Whites-only referendum leads to a 69 per cent vote to continue reforms.
1993
Nelson Mandela and President F W de Klerk share the Nobel Peace Prize.
1994
Democratic elections in April; ANC president Nelson Mandela elected President of South Africa. South Africa re-enters the Commonwealth.
1995
Rugby World Cup held in South Africa. The Queen visits.

Top left: the Voortrekkers on their epic Great Trek
Below: scene from the Anglo-Boer War

THE SECOND ANGLO-BOER WAR

Following success in the First Anglo-Boer War (1880), the ZAR regained independence from Britain. By then its gold was attracting droves of foreign prospectors. British imperialists instigated the Jameson Raid (1895), hoping to ignite an uprising followed by the installation of a British administration. Its failure and ensuing events led to the Second Boer War (1899). President Kruger's commandos beat the British at Talana Hill and routed them at Nicholson's Nek, but their siege of Ladysmith was disastrous and cost them the war. By 1900 Pretoria had surrendered. A rural guerilla war resulted in savage retribution: Boer women and children were imprisoned in the world's first concentration camps. The horror of these led ultimately to the Peace of Vereeniging (1902).

Politics

South Africa is going through a period of profound transformation, with a new flag, a second national anthem to join the existing one, and a brand new constitution in the making. Democracy has replaced apartheid, leaving the government a formidable task: to redress the gross inequality endemic in South African society.

The demise of apartheid

Apartheid brought South Africa to its knees. Vilified by the international community, smitten by problems arising from unemployment, townships on the boil, decline in white standards of living and a state of emergency, by the end of the 1980s it was apparent, even to conservative whites, that change was inevitable.

Violent demonstrations like this one at Uitenhage characterised the 1980s

In 1989 President P W Botha was replaced by the pragmatist F W de Klerk who, although a conservative, understood the apocalyptic alternative. On 2 February 1990, at his first parliamentary session as president, he announced the unbanning of the ANC (African National Congress), the South African Communist Party and the Pan-African Congress, a radical movement that broke away from the ANC in 1959. Nelson Mandela and hundreds of other political prisoners were to be freed. Thus

The flag of the New South Africa symbolises the hopes for unity of most of the nation

he paved the way for a black-led South Africa. Discussions with the ANC to negotiate the revolution from apartheid to democracy had begun four years before Mandela's release and were to lead to one of modern history's most remarkable political transformations. De Klerk's speech shocked Parliament; in just 35 minutes he turned three centuries of white rule upside down.

The years of protest

Protest, often violent, played a key role in setting in motion the wheels of reform. The Sharpeville Massacre (1960), in which police fired on demonstrators, killing 69, released a wave of revulsion throughout the international community. The era of political isolation and violent racial conflict began. In the same year the ANC and other black liberation organisations were banned, and the ANC's armed wing, UmKhonto we Sizwe (Spear of the Nation) was launched, its aim a programme of sabotage. This led, in 1964, to the Rivonia Treason Trial and Mandela's arrest with other ANC leaders.

In the 1960s and '70s various attempts were made by leaders B J Vorster (1966–78) and P W Botha (1978–90) to stop the rot, but 'reforms' were half-hearted: Botha's amendment of the constitution allowed Indians and Coloureds limited say in government, but black Africans were excluded. In 1976, a student demonstration in Soweto against the use of Afrikaans as a medium of instruction in black segregated schools triggered a violent uprising which, lasting a year, left over 600 dead. Then in 1977, Steve Biko, founder of the radical 'black consciousness' movement, died in police custody in suspicious circumstances. By the mid-1980s the turmoil had reached such a degree that Mandela, in gaol, decided that the time was right for the ANC to take the initiative and open a dialogue with the government.

> 'If Nelson Mandela, like Jomo Kenyatta, goes to prison, comes back and rules South Africa, then I say God forbid.'
>
> PRIME MINISTER VERWOERD
> on dispatching Mandela to jail for life, 1964

The Government of National Unity

In 1991, against a backdrop of violence and political infighting, a negotiation process was set in motion. It resulted in an interim constitution, a National Assembly of 400 members elected by universal franchise, and a federal framework of nine provincial assemblies. A final agreement, in November 1993, provided for a temporary (5-year)

F W de Klerk and Nelson Mandela

Government of National Unity, a coalition of all parties that won more than 5 per cent of the vote in the election of April 1994. Working towards a next general election in 1999, it will produce a final constitution and a comprehensive Bill of Rights.

In the Government of National Unity, parties are awarded cabinet seats in proportion to their strength. The 1994 election left the ANC with a 62 per cent majority in the National Assembly, clear majorities in six of the provincial legislatures and a slender majority in a seventh, while Chief Mangosuthu Buthelezi's Inkatha Freedom Party won

NELSON MANDELA

For millions of ordinary people, Nelson Mandela stands for dignity and rights and a better future. His name has travelled the world as a symbol of freedom. Mandela was born in 1918 in Transkei in the Eastern Cape. In 1944 he helped form the youth league of the ANC with Oliver Tambo and Walter Sisulu, and in 1958 he married Winnie Madakizela. After the ANC was banned in 1961, he lived for 17 months as a fugitive, evading arrest until 1962 when he was jailed for five years. He was later charged under the Suppression of Communism Act and in 1964, after the eight-month Rivonia Trial, he was sentenced to life imprisonment. On 11 February 1990 he was released, and in 1994 was elected President of South Africa. In the tense months leading up to its first democratic elections, South Africa teetered on the brink of civil war, yet millions voted, white politics in alliance with the black cause. The man responsible for managing this compromise was Mandela.

the province of KwaZulu/Natal and F W de Klerk's National Party the Western Cape. The leader of the majority party, the ANC, is president, and there are two deputy presidents – one from the party running second and the other from any other party gaining more than 20 per cent of the vote, or, if no party achieved this, from the majority party.

Apartheid

*A*partheid – segregation and separate development of the races – was not an invention of the Afrikaners as many people think. Conversely, the British tradition in South Africa was by no means non-racial and democratic: many of the apartheid laws passed by the National Party in the 1950s were based on existing laws, in many cases simply tightening or tidying them.

But it was Jan Smuts's Native Affairs Act of 1920 that took the first step towards implementation of political segregation in the Union of South Africa. It established the principle that African political activity should be divorced from 'white' South Africa and ushered in a period of intense debate on 'native policy', during which state ideology was refined and clarified.

When the National Party under Dr D F Malan won the 1948 election on the platform of apartheid, they immediately adopted it as a national political programme, bringing in many new laws. Sex outside marriage between races was already banned, but the 1949 Mixed Marriages Act and the Immorality Act of the following year banned any sex between races. Laws allowing Africans into urban areas were redefined; Africans had to carry a pass and failure to do so was a criminal offence. 'Group Areas' defined as White, Black, Indian or Coloured (mixed-race) made separation absolute. On the crucial issue of land, the Prevention of Illegal Squatting Act gave the government power to move African tenants from privately or publicly owned land. This was only completion of legislation which had begun with Cecil John Rhodes, prime minister of the Cape Colony from 1890 to 1895.

For 30 years the National Party government wrestled with the implementation of apartheid, but under political, economic, military and diplomatic pressure they finally abandoned it in 1990. Today, the Party explains it away as an experiment that did not work. And yet the cynicism with which Africans, Coloureds and Asians were deprived of civic and human rights, and the callous way in which apartheid was implemented, puts apartheid in the same historical category as Nazism, Fascism and state Communism.

A sign of former times

Culture and People

South Africa's population of nearly 40 million is distinguished by its cultural diversity. More than a third lives in and around the cities and towns, mostly in the overcrowded former townships. The replacement of white minority rule by black majority rule without civil war is arguably one of the strangest events in a country whose history is one of racial conflict.

Asians

Around one million Asians live in South Africa. Originally recruited to work on the sugar plantations of Natal, the country's Indian population is today largely confined to the KwaZulu/Natal province. The Indians speak Gujarati, Urdu, Tamil or Hindi. Most practise the Hindu religion. A generally prosperous group, many retain the traditions and customs of India itself. The Cape Muslims (or Malays) are based mostly in and around Cape Town, descendants of slaves or of political and religious exiles from Ceylon (now Sri Lanka), Java, Sumatra and Bali. Their distinctive cuisine and cultural traditions are part of the fabric of Cape Town.

Blacks

There are around 30 million blacks in South Africa. Most belong to the Nguni or Sotho groups of peoples. Of the Nguni, the Zulu, Xhosa, Ndebele and Swazi are dominant and, of the Sotho, the Northern Sotho, Southern Sotho and Venda predominate. Although most live in rural areas, the drift to the cities and the influence of western culture is destroying many traditions.

Coloureds

Accounting for nearly 12 per cent of the population, 'Coloured' describes mixed-race people of European, Asiatic and indigenous descent. The term is a creation of apartheid. Culturally associated with the whites, the Coloureds are concentrated in and around Cape Town and in the Western Cape. A supreme irony is that, although the former white government discriminated against them, most Coloureds – who tend to look down on the blacks – voted for the Nationalist Party in the 1994 elections.

Economically marginalised, their main concern under the ANC government is the affirmative action programme which, they claim, is designed to favour blacks.

Craftswomen at work in the Drakensberg

Zulu mother and child. A proud people, the Zulu cling tenaciously to their tribal identity

HOMELANDS

The Zulu are concentrated in KwaZulu/Natal. Under apartheid, KwaZulu was one of the tribal 'Homelands' – a political invention designed to keep blacks 'out' of South Africa. Centred on the traditional lands of tribal groups, they were supposed to be self-sufficient and self-governing. Millions were forcibly dispossessed and resettled there, the Xhosa to Transkei and Ciskei, the Ndebele to KwaNdebele, and the Venda people to Venda. Bophuthatswana was for the Tswana. This policy, now abolished, caused untold misery and is partly responsible for the drift to urban areas and its associated problems – lack of housing, unemployment, and so on. It is hoped the democratisation of South Africa will lead to a fundamental transformation of the lives of South Africa's blacks.

Whites

Of the nearly 5 million whites, most are either English or Afrikaans-speaking, with the latter in the majority. Most of the English-speakers are of British extraction. The Afrikaners, however, are an ethnic mix of Dutch, German, French, British, and, whatever they may say to the contrary, black and Coloured. The white population also includes Portuguese from Angola and Mozambique, Germans, Dutch, Italians, Greeks and a large second- or third-generation Jewish population from Eastern Europe.

From 1948 the Afrikaners had the upper hand, and the English-speakers, traditionally liberal, for the most part remained politically impotent. Today white South Africans are still adjusting to majority rule. They still hold the real economic power and, when asked to justify their determination to keep it, simply shrug their shoulders and point to the sad mismanagement and corruption in much of the rest of black Africa.

Above: a vibrantly decorated Ndebele house
Left: ostrich egg encased in colourful beadwork

Religion

South Africa is predominantly Christian. Many Afrikaners hold a fundamental belief that South Africa was the God-given Promised Land and this fact alone sanctioned the Great Trek, the massacre of the black tribes at Blood River, and much more. Biggest of the Christian groups is that of the Dutch Reformed Churches to which most Afrikaners and many Coloureds belong, but there are also large Roman Catholic, Methodist, Anglican, Presbyterian and Baptist congregations. Of these, the Anglicans have the highest profile due to the colourful persona of Archbishop Desmond Tutu, a leading campaigner for reform.

There are over 120,000 Jews, while 70 per cent of the Indian population is Hindu and virtually all of the rest Muslim. A minority of blacks follow traditional religions and practices – some involving ancestor worship – while others belong to churches which have combined aspects of Christianity with elements of traditional belief.

African culture

Traditional culture in rural areas is still strong, but scattered and detribalised black South Africans, mingling in often hostile urban areas, are seeing their old traditions fade and die or spawn new forms. The various black cultural groups share broad similarities in language, folklore, dress and regalia, etiquette, religion, hereditary rank, bonds of kinship, and concepts of property and land ownership. All are based on beliefs in a masculine deity, ancestral spirits and various supernatural forces. Marriage customs and taboos differ: among the Nguni a fear of incest prohibits marriage to a relative while the Sotho can marry cousins. Marriages are arranged by the family, polygamy is permitted and a dowry is usually paid even among urban dwellers (though hard cash generally replaces cattle in those situations). First-born males have inheritance rights.

Speaking with beads

The beadwork designs, particularly of the Ndebele, Zulu and Xhosa, have evolved from a tradition of craft skills developed over many generations. The major preoccupation with beadwork today dates from white settlement, but east-coast glass beads, derived from Arab and – from the 16th century – Portuguese sources, were imported via the trade routes that crossed the Transvaal from at least the end of the first millennium.

Originally, beads of unbaked clay and metal were made and worn singly or on chains. This tradition, upgraded and streamlined, has been reinterpreted in the 20th century. In some cases African beadwork has even entered the realms of international high fashion. Jewellery and ornamental headdresses indicate age, status and the area from which the wearer originates; they can even send coded love messages.

Women

Women's status varies from group to group. Men certainly hold dominance among some native groups, but other tribal societies are matrilineal, with women exerting real influence on how things are run. In modern South Africa, many younger white women work, as do a great many urban black women, the latter mostly as domestic or factory workers.

There is no doubt that women's lives are often hard. In some groups, men can have many wives, but women only one husband, and sometimes a widow is 'inherited' by her brother-in-law. The women of warrior tribes, most notably the Zulu, were traditionally left behind for long periods by their husbands. This pattern has continued in modern society, with men going off to find work in the cities and mines while their womenfolk run the household in the village. They keep the family going, tend livestock and pay the taxes. They rely on sporadic allowances or eke out a living from vegetable plots. Often the men never return, having started a new family.

Today women make up the majority of the population in rural areas. Their isolation and poverty has militated against the pooling of their resources and fighting for a better deal, but now the interim constitution contains an equality clause making it possible for women to challenge any law that discriminates against them.

Geography

South Africa is washed by the Atlantic Ocean on the west and the Indian Ocean on the east and has land boundaries with Namibia, Botswana, Zimbabwe, Mozambique and Swaziland. Notwithstanding divergent political development, all these countries share many physical, cultural, demographic and economic features. South Africa is the powerhouse and larder.

THE LIE OF THE LAND

Much of southern Africa forms part of a vast plateau which stretches north across East Africa to the Red Sea.

The coastal belt

South Africa's coastal belt is narrow, extending below sea-level to form a continental shelf. In the west, coasts are rocky and, going north, arid. Here the water is chilled by the Benguela Current. In the south and east, where the landscape is lush, and the northeast, where it is tropical, coasts are washed by the warm Mozambique Current.

The escarpment

Separating the coastal areas from the interior plateau are high escarpments, at their most magnificent in the Drakensberg Mountain range bordering KwaZulu/Natal and Lesotho, the highest mountains in southern Africa. On Mont-aux-Sources rise eight of the country's rivers.

The interior plateau

The South African part of this plateau is shaped like a saucer, its rim the escarpment which slopes inward to the Kalahari Basin straddling the Northern Cape's border with Namibia. At its southern extremity are the dry plains of the Great Karoo, which covers much of the interior. The climate is harsh and the rainfall limited. Population is scarce.

Highveld and Lowveld

Along its eastern and northeastern sides stretch the grasslands of the Highveld. In

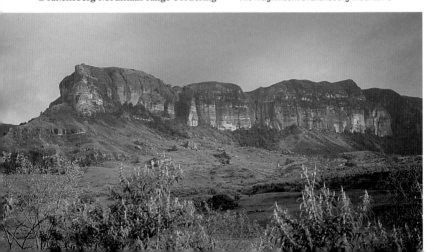

The magnificent Drakensberg Mountains

The unmistakable profile of Table Mountain, with Cape Town spread around its foot

Gauteng, at a height of almost 1,750m, is Johannesburg. Due east, the escarpment drops about 1,000m through cliffs, buttresses and magnificent river valleys to the Lowveld plain. This is savannah country, for many the true landscape of Africa. A large chunk encompasses the Kruger National Park.

Africa's tip
At the bottom of the continent, the Cape Peninsula's Cape Point is not Africa's southernmost tip. Cape Agulhas, about 200km southeast, has that distinction, presiding over the meeting of the Indian and Atlantic Oceans. Running parallel to the southern coast are magnificent mountain ranges – Swartberg, Tsitsikamma, Outeniqua and Langeberg – and, closer to Cape Town, the Hottentots-Holland and Drakenstein ranges, and, in the city, Table Mountain. On the west coast is the Cedarberg.

LAND AND WATER
Conditions in South Africa are generally dry, and there are few natural forests or lakes. With water limited, conservation and supply receive high priority. There are over 300 large dams, the largest

constructed in two major river systems: the Orange-Vaal, draining the plateau, and the Tugela. These, and other rivers, are linked by canals and pumping schemes to supply water to the country's expanding urban areas.

NATURAL RESOURCES
The South African plateau is composed of the oldest and most stable rock formations on earth. Part of this, in the Witwatersrand, the southern Transvaal and the northern Free State, is famous for gold, silver and uranium, while scarce metals like platinum and chrome are mined in the Bushveld Igneous Complex stretching across central Transvaal into the Northwest. A variety of minerals including copper, iron, lead, tin and zinc are exploited all over the Transvaal and the Northern Cape. Less ancient rocks are associated with the coalfields of the Eastern Transvaal, the northern Free State and northern KwaZulu/Natal, and with the volcanic diamond pipes of Kimberley and Cullinan (near Pretoria). These rich deposits were the ancient sources of the alluvial diamond fields of the Northern Cape's and Namibia's Atlantic coast.

Fauna

South Africa is still the home of a rich and diverse community of animals, though theirs is a shrinking world. Since the first pioneers arrived ecosystems have been disrupted, species have become extinct and game has retreated into ever smaller territories. Nevertheless, in the mammal class, for example, there are today more than 30 species of antelope alone. Birds are even more varied, and over a quarter of the world's land tortoise species are found here.

The Cape vulture relies on its amazing eyesight to spot carcasses below

South Africa's game and nature reserves are considered one of the country's most valuable resources, and there are many in virtually every region. Unusually for Africa, certain species are expanding – elephant, lion, leopard and white rhino – and excess animals are being sold to other countries whose numbers have been depleted. South Africa is one of the greatest places for game-spotting, and the chances of seeing the 'Big Five' (lion, elephant, leopard, buffalo and black or white rhino) are high.

BIRDS

Of some 900 bird species occurring in South Africa, 113 are endemic. The variety is enormous, from the ostrich, the world's largest bird, to the spectacular fish and crowned eagles, the nectar-eating green lourie or long-tailed sugar bird, the crowned crane and the jackass penguin of the Cape's western coast. Some are easily viewed in reserves, others are restricted to particular localities. Many game birds are seen at the roadside; telephone wires and poles provide convenient perches, and smaller animals and reptiles killed by traffic provide rich pickings. Keen birdwatchers should travel with a copy of *South African Birds* by Ian Sinclair (Struik, 1990), and a pair of binoculars.

MARINE LIFE

South Africa's seas maintain a huge variety of creatures and plants. The east coast's warm Mozambique Current and the west coast's cold Benguela Current provide widely varying habitats. Dolphins, sharks, seals and whales are common, often seen in the Cape Peninsula's False Bay area, and in Walker Bay (Hermanus) at the heart of the so-called whale route extending from St Helena Bay on the west coast to Tsitsikamma beyond Plettenberg Bay on the south coast. Southern right whales (*Eubalaena australis*), which can grow to a length of 16m, arrive in May and stay

A southern fur sea-lion

until November having calved, as do the humpback whales (*Megaptera novaeangliae*), which are renowned for their acrobatic dexterity, and the Bryde's whale (*Balaenoptera edeni*). Some killer whales (*Orcinus orca*), actually members of the dolphin family, are resident year-round in southern Africa's waters.

A whale-watching hotline provides up-to-the-minute information on the whereabouts of the whales (tel: 0283–22629 or 21475).

THE COELACANTH

In 1938 the modern world's first coelacanth (*Latimeria chalumnae*) was caught off East London's coast. Believed to have been extinct for some 80 million years, and known only from fossil remains, it is a primitive fish whose fins resemble stump-like legs. The East London Museum (see page 56) has a specimen on display.

MAMMALS

South Africa is vast, and the number of mammals it supports huge. Here is a selection of those you might see.

Antelope

Bontebok *Damaliscus dorcas dorcas*
Virtually extinct by the middle of the 19th century when it was decided to preserve this distinctive animal, the bontebok is confined to an area between Bredasdorp and Cape Agulhas in the Western Cape. It has an unbroken light blaze from forehead to muzzle.

Bushbuck *Tragelaphus scriptus*
This pugnacious little animal, recognisable by the white spots on its flanks, favours forested country and dense bush close to water. Only males have horns (up to 30cm in length). Bushbuck are dangerous when cornered.

Blue wildebeest form huge herds

Cheetahs at rest. These elegant cats usually hunt in the early morning or late evening

Duiker

The fawny-grey common, or grey duiker (*Sylvicapra grimmia*) is widely seen in open countryside from semi-desert to mountainous areas. Growing to 60cm tall, it is very adaptable, and may even be found in gardens or cultivated land. The red duiker (*Cephalophus natalensis*), inhabits forested country and is rarer, while the blue duiker (*Cephalophus monticola*) is most reclusive of all. Generally solitary, they also form temporary pairs, their favoured habitat dense woodland.

Eland *Taurotragus oryx*

This, the largest antelope, is easily tamed. Quite common, it may be seen in large herds on open plains or gently wooded areas. Though ox-like, it is able to leap to a height of 2.5m.

Gemsbok *Oryx gazella*

Living in large herds on dry plains and semi-desert areas, the gemsbok is noted for its splendid horns. The males' are straight while the females', longer and more slender, may be slightly curved. It has a black and white face, pale grey body, and black and white underbelly and legs.

Impala *Aepyceros melampus*

Growing to about 1m high at the shoulder, the impala is found in large herds in the savannah and scrub grassland. It can leap a distance of 10m and clear a height of 3m. The males have long lyre-shaped horns. Russet-coloured with paler sides, it has a white underbelly and black stripes on tail and rump.

Klipspringer *Oreotragus oreotragus*

The small klipspringer is a mountain-dweller, its rubbery hooves giving good grip on steep slopes. The males have short horns, the females are hornless. Pale tawny with a whitish underbelly.

Kudu *Tragelaphus strepsiceros*

This handsome, timid beast, with white stripes on its flanks, is found in bushy country close to water. The male has extravagantly twisted horns while the female is hornless. The bulls are often solitary.

The powerful and dangerous Cape buffalo

Red hartebeest *Alcelaphus buselaphus*
Once close to extinction, this large and
distinctive animal has been reintroduced
into its traditional territory – the arid
Northern Cape and Namibia. Tan with
ridged horns.

Reedbuck
The southern or common reedbuck
(*Redunca arundinum*) usually lives close to
water, in open, lightly-wooded areas.
They are usually found alone or in pairs,
and occasionally in small groups. The
grey mountain reedbuck (*Redunca
fulvorufula*) lives on rocky mountain
slopes and is found in larger groups. Both
species are shy and alert. The females are
hornless and, in the case of the mountain
reedbuck, larger than the male.

Springbok *Antidorcas marsupialis*
The only gazelle found south of the
Zambezi River is fairly common in South
Africa – and is the national emblem.
Found on dry, open plains, often in large
herds, when running it frequently leaps

into the air. Tan with white underbelly,
and white and tan face.

Steenbok *Raphicerus campestris*
Widespread across the country, the little
red-brown steenbok is a solitary animal
that favours flat, open plains.

Plains animals
Buffalo *Syncerus caffer*
This irascible beast is huge, with heavy
horn bosses, bad sight and terrible
hearing, but an excellent sense of smell.
Males are black and females tinged
brown. It occurs in small groups in a
variety of habitats, usually close to water.

Cheetah *Acinonyx jubatus*
Living in the open country, in the
Kalahari and the northeastern Transvaal,
the cheetah, recognisable from its
distinctive black spots, is the world's
fastest land mammal, capable of speeds
of at least 80kph. It has a small head and
long limbs, and lives in small groups,
hunting mainly early in the morning.

Elephant *Loxodonta africana*
The largest of land mammals grows to a height of 3.3m. It eats leaves, grass, bark and reeds, lives in herds and is highly intelligent. The single calf born is suckled for two years. Elephants have adapted to a variety of different habitats, and can be found in open plains as well as dense forest. Male tusks are longer than the females', and can grow to 3m.

Giraffe *Giraffa camelopardalis*
Living in small herds in open woodland, the giraffe can go without water for long periods. It is distinguished by its neck which, despite its enormous length, has only seven cervical vertebrae. The giraffe's main diet is acacia foliage. Males are up to 6m tall, females 4.5m.

Hippopotamus *Hippopotamus amphibius*
The comic-looking hippo is a monster if disturbed. It can deliver a nasty bite, tip a canoe or, worse, chomp it in half. Hugely gregarious, it swims well and can

AFRICA'S ELEPHANTS
A century ago there were at least three million elephants in Africa. By 1981 there were just 1.2 million and eight years later the population had dropped to some 622,000. Nowadays, there are thought to be less than half a million and numbers are still declining in most countries, the terrible result of the human population explosion, the associated destruction of the elephant's habitat and migration routes, and, above all, the trade in ivory, the 'white gold' of Africa. Only South Africa has a growing elephant population, so successful that even after exporting live animals to other countries, culling is a sad necessity to stop them turning the landscape to a desert, and only South Africa has, as yet, escaped the worst attentions of the poachers. The South Africans understandably want permission to sell a priceless ivory stockpile and believe that a carefully controlled ivory 'harvest' will ensure the long-term survival of the elephant. Further north, they have seen the devastation caused by the illegal trade which accompanies any open market.

remain submerged for up to 5 minutes. A herbivore, it emerges at night from the water to graze, consuming up to 180kg of food a day.

Hyena
Large and dog-like, the spotted hyena (*Crocuta crocuta*) is found in the savannah regions of the Eastern Transvaal and Northern Province. It is more handsome

Deceptively docile – a male lion at rest

A family of elephants. Such groups of females and calves are led by a matriarch

than the brown hyena (*Hyaena brunnea*) but both have a high front and a low rump. Hyenas are scavengers, though the spotted variety attack large game.

Leopard *Panthera pardus*
The leopard is highly dangerous if confronted. Rarely seen, it hunts at night, monkeys and baboons being a favourite meal. It occurs in many wild areas of the country and also in closer proximity to people, sometimes visiting farms or even towns. It is recognisable by its coat of clustered rings of dark spots.

Lion *Panthera leo*
Favouring open, bushy countryside, lions live in prides of 10 to 20 animals. The largest of Africa's cats, the males have thick manes and are most active at night. Most of the hunting for the pride is done by the females acting in unison.

Rhinoceros
These huge, ungainly beasts, much valued for their horn, are under tremendous threat in southern Africa. Relatively shy, they generally live alone. The black rhinoceros (*Diceros bicornis*) is immensely aggressive. The white, or square-lipped rhinoceros (*Ceratotherium simum*) is not in fact white (both species are the same colour); its name derives from the Dutch word *weit* ('wide') after its wide mouth, distinct from the black rhino's pointed mouth with prehensile upper lip.

Wildebeest
The blue wildebeest (*Connochaetes taurinus*) has smaller hindquarters than the black wildebeest (*Connochaetes gnou*), which is distinguished by a long tail, dark at the base and almost pure white above. Both have massive shoulders and curved horns and are generally seen in open grassy plains in large herds.

Zebra
Burchell's zebra (*Equus burchelli*) is a noisy beast commonly found in northern KwaZulu/Natal and the Eastern Transvaal in groups of up to 20. The Cape mountain zebra (*Equus zebra zebra*) is an endangered species. Found in the Eastern Cape (and protected in the Mountain Zebra National Park), it is smaller than the Burchell's variety, has a distinctive dewlap and sports a gridiron.

The gently smiling jaws of *Crocodylus niloticus*, now rare in the wild in South Africa

Primates
Chacma Baboon *Papio ursinus*
Most commonly seen by the roadside in mountain areas in bands of up to 20 or more, the baboon can deliver a nasty bite. Do not feed it.

Vervet Monkey *Cercopithecus pygerythrus*
Found in dense bush chattering noisily, its preferred habitat is the eastern coastal zone. Unafraid of man, vervet monkeys are recognisable by their dark faces outlined in white.

REPTILES
Snakes, lizards, tortoises and crocodiles are well represented in South Africa. They live and survive in some unlikely habitats.

Crocodiles (*Crocodylus niloticus*) are found in game reserves and – in the north of KwaZulu/Natal – occasionally in the wild. Some reptiles, like the **geometric tortoise** (*Psammobates geometricus*) – so-called because of the intricate patterns on its shell – are endangered species. Others, mostly snakes, are venomous. There is also an eccentric array of lizards and leguaans, the most astonishing of which is the

water leguaan (*Varanus niloticus*), or Nile monitor, which grows up to 2m in length.

Snakes
The **boomslang** (*Dispholidus typus*) is a greenish colour and is widespread except in drier areas. It glides through trees and bushes and is a good swimmer. Numerous and even more widespread, the sluggish **puff-adder** (*Bitis arietans*) is easily stepped on; its bite is often fatal. The **Cape cobra** (*Naja nivea*) found in the Cape, the Free State and the southwestern Transvaal, is extremely venomous. Golden-brown to blackish, it swims and climbs and is often found near water. The **spitting cobra** (*Hemachatus haemachatus*), or rinkals, spits venom over 2m; if surprised, it will rear up and expand its hood. The **black mamba** (*Dendroaspis polylepis*), in fact greenish-black, is found in KwaZulu/Natal and the Transvaal and, like the **green mamba** (*Dendroaspis angusticeps*), is extremely poisonous. The **common African python** (*Python sebae*), one of the world's largest snakes, occurs in KwaZulu/Natal and the Transvaal. It is not venomous, but can still deliver a nasty bite.

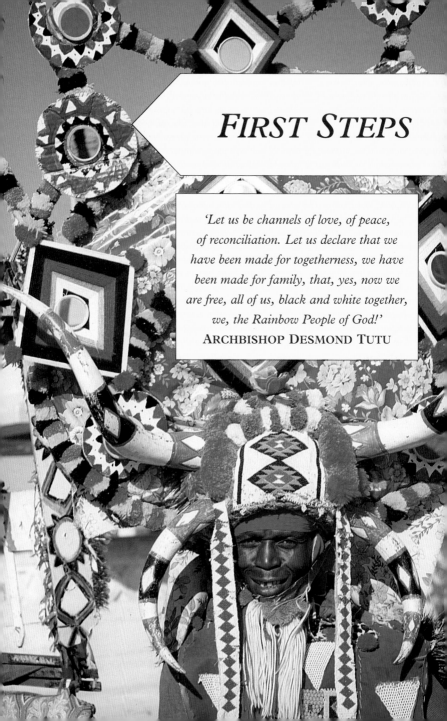

FIRST STEPS

'Let us be channels of love, of peace, of reconciliation. Let us declare that we have been made for togetherness, we have been made for family, that, yes, now we are free, all of us, black and white together, we, the Rainbow People of God!'
ARCHBISHOP DESMOND TUTU

First Steps

South Africa is mainly a fly-drive destination, and many tour operators offer tailor-made itineraries. It is also the perfect place for a 'two-centre' holiday: combine a laid-back beach sojourn with a trip to a game reserve. To help you plan your itinerary, the best destinations for a variety of interests are listed below.

Architecture
Cape Town, Graaff-Reinet, Stellenbosch, Swellendam and Tulbagh for Cape Dutch architecture; KwaZulu/Natal for Zulu tribal buildings; Mpumalanga (Eastern Transvaal) for decorated Ndebele homesteads; Bathurst and Grahamstown for Georgian Colonial; Pietermaritzburg, Cape Town and Oudtshoorn for Victorian.

Beaches
The country's best beaches are located around the Cape Peninsula, at Hermanus, along the Garden Route, and on the north and south coasts of KwaZulu/Natal. On the West Coast are Langebaan and St Helena Bay.

Fishing
There's trout fishing in the foothills of the Transvaal Drakensberg and the Natal Midlands, while the coasts of KwaZulu/Natal and the Western Cape are best for deep-sea and game fishing.

Food
Cape Town, Durban, Johannesburg and Pretoria.

Game-viewing
The best all-round game reserves are the Kruger National Park and the Hluhluwe-Umfolozi Game Reserve. Some private game parks offer concentrations of game in smaller areas. Others, such as Londolozi, Mala Mala and Sabi Sabi share an open border with the Kruger.

Hiking and adventure
Of the country's many mountain ranges, the Drakensberg and the Cedarberg offer some of the best hikes and climbs. In the city, nothing can beat Table Mountain and the mountains of the Cape Peninsula. The most rugged national parks lie in the Northern Cape. The best is the Richtersveld National Park; a visit requires the services of a guide.

History
Cape Town, Stellenbosch and Grahamstown for settler history; Johannesburg for pioneers of the gold rush; Kimberley for the history of diamonds; KwaZulu/Natal and the Free State for battlefields of Black, Boer and British wars; KwaZulu/Natal for Shaka and Zulu history.

Nightlife
Cape Town, Durban and Johannesburg.

Tribal peoples
KwaZulu/Natal for the Zulu; Northern Province for the Venda; Eastern Cape for the Xhosa; Eastern Transvaal Highveld for the Ndebele.

Whale-watching
Cape Peninsula beaches and Hermanus.

Wild flowers
Namaqualand and the west coast of the Northern Cape – but only in the spring.

Taking in one of South Africa's spectacular views

WHEN TO GO
Cape Town and the southernmost part of the Western Cape have a Mediterranean climate with mild, changeable winters, when most of the rainfall occurs, and a warm to hot summer. Durban and the KwaZulu/Natal coast enjoy a subtropical climate, with plenty of sunshine all year round. The winters in the interior are dry and warm, although it may get chilly at night; summers are hot with more rain.

Peak holiday season is Christmas and January, when most South Africans take their long holiday, often in the Cape. Schools and colleges close, hotel prices rise with rooms at a premium, and roads become more dangerous. The Lowveld is uncomfortably hot and in Mpumalanga (Eastern Transvaal) and KwaZulu/Natal humidity is a problem. In February the weather is lovely, and there are fewer people competing for hotel beds. To view game, wait until autumn or even winter, when less foliage enables better visibility.

WHAT TO TAKE
Most things are available in South Africa, but serious hikers should take walking boots that have already been 'broken in'. Budget travellers should bring sleeping bags, and everybody should bring a pair of binoculars.

GETTING AROUND
Urban public transport is shoddy, but intercity coaches and trains are exceptionally efficient (coach travel is cheaper). For long distances air travel is preferable.

By air
Most bigger towns have an airport and the range of scheduled flights connecting them is very comprehensive.

By rail

South Africa has a major network of long distance railway routes, and going by train is a good way of seeing the landscape at a leisurely pace.

By road

The road network is excellent and generally well maintained. You do need a car in South Africa as public transport is neither reliable nor comprehensive.

For more on travel see pages 182–3.

SAFETY AND SECURITY

The intention is not to cast a pall of gloom over holiday prospects, but to put travellers on their guard: violence in South Africa remains at a high level, and most of it is criminal rather than political. Take sensible precautions; be as vigilant as you would anywhere else. Although criminal activity is concentrated in urban areas, take time to listen to local advice wherever you go.

Some key rules

• Avoid townships and surrounding areas unless travelling with a legitimate and escorted tour. Never go into a township at night, and never go alone.
• Travel long distances in daylight hours if possible and don't pick up hitchhikers.
• Be alert for muggers, notably in city centres, and particularly in downtown Johannesburg, where knife-point muggings occur even in broad daylight on busy streets.
• Before going to isolated beaches, particularly in the Eastern Cape and northern KwaZulu/Natal, check that they are safe.
• In the car at night, always keep the doors locked. In ill-lit urban areas where people are milling about, use your judgment before responding if someone accosts you. Park in well-lit areas.
• At night, if you feel unsafe when waiting at a red light, it is perfectly acceptable to continue on your way provided the road is clear.
• Leave jewellery, watches and expensive video or camera equipment in the hotel. Never travel with travellers' cheques or large amounts of cash.
• Visiting the beach, leave all your valuables behind and only take the minimum of cash for your day's needs.
• Never leave valuables lying in the back of the car.
• In rented houses and lower-floor hotel rooms, in the absence of burglar bars keep windows closed at night.

SURVIVING IN THE WILDS

Follow a few ground rules and you won't be confronted by a rapacious lion or find yourself being driven at speed to the nearest hospital, the victim of a nasty snakebite. Always be prepared,

Beach at Mossel Bay on the Cape's Garden Route, one of South Africa's most scenic drives

and take advice on the right clothes to wear and what to take with you.

Some tips
• Do some homework to be able to identify the most dangerous snakes – snakebite treatment varies according to species. If you stumble on a snake, never provoke it. If bitten, get immediate help. Wear long trousers and closed shoes out in the bush. At night hang your shoes upside down.
• Check your body for ticks after venturing into the bush. Their bites can cause illness: headaches, hot and cold sweats and fever. If this happens, see a doctor.
• If visiting the Transvaal Lowveld, the Kruger National Park and KwaZulu/Natal, take a course of anti-malaria tablets before starting out.
• Bilharzia, a waterborne sickness caused by a parasitical worm and spread by snails, is common in the northern and eastern regions. Do not swim without assurances that the water is unaffected.

• Always take a water bottle with you on hikes and trails, and something warm to wear for the evening.
• Before making a trip out into the wilds, or up into the mountains, always tell somebody where you are going.
• Out camping, shake out your sleeping bag before you get in. Snakes, scorpions and spiders have been known to creep in.
• Never feed wild animals, never approach them and, particularly in the case of baboons and other monkeys, never look them in the eye. Never get out of the car near wild animals – even the humble bushbuck has caused several human fatalities.
• It may not be a good idea to swim from empty beaches.
• Take an insulation blanket made of foil. It could be a useful accessory for cold nights or a life-saver for accident victims. A supply of aspirin, tablets for purifying water, anti-histamines for any allergic reaction (after a bite), insect repellent, sun-block and first-aid dressings would be a good idea too.

LANGUAGE

English and Afrikaans were the country's official languages in the past. Indeed anything associated with government, like signs or brochures, is still in both languages, and English is widely spoken. Now there are 11 official languages: English, Afrikaans, Ndebele, Northern Sotho, Southern Sotho, Swati, Tsonga, Tswana, Venda, Xhosa and Zulu. Eight are spoken by more than one million people. Zulu is the first or home language spoken by 22 per cent of the people, Xhosa by 17 per cent, Afrikaans by 15 per cent and English by only 9 per cent. Afrikaans, which derives from the Dutch of the earliest settlers, is the language of the Coloured people as well as the Afrikaners, and for many others, both black and white, it is a second language. There are various Indian languages and plenty of dialects within languages. In the townships, to communicate across cultural divides, a Zulu-Xhosa combination with a bit of Sotho thrown in is called Fanagalo, and is fairly widespread in the mines.

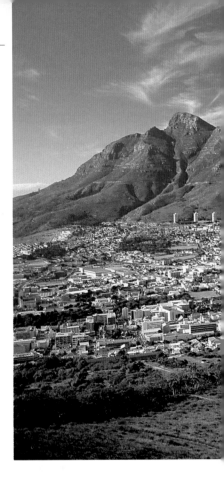

ETIQUETTE
The greeting

On the whole, South Africans are a warm people. Strangers acknowledge each other in the street and there are nearly as many ways of greeting as there are different cultural groups. In general, the ritual is not too different from Western experience. However, whereas people in the West are used to a hurried 'good morning' – if they greet each other at all – black Africans take more time over it and pass a few minutes together in pleasant exchange. Many South Africans exchange a kiss with familiars, either on the cheek or the lips.

The handshake

The handshake is a familiar form of greeting. When meeting someone for the first time, or renewing an acquaintance, this is fairly common – essential in business situations. The African handshake is a variation: this entails shaking hands in the usual way then, without letting go of the other person's hand, slipping your hand around each other's thumbs then back into the traditional grasp.

Hospitality

Among whites, Western-style hospitality prevails and is particularly lavish in

Some two million people inhabit Cape Town, a small city with a beautiful setting

Afrikaans homes. Newcomers are bombarded with invitations to swim or eat. Wherever you go, whether into black or white homes, always take something. Some homes in South Africa are very poor indeed and a guest's gift to the host or hostess never goes amiss – though a South African white male wouldn't be seen dead clutching a bunch of flowers.

Dress

The South African lifestyle is fairly casual: it's too hot to be otherwise. Social occasions – weddings, dinner parties – require a modicum of formality (men should take a light jacket or smart trousers), and businessmen may be expected to wear a tie. The current trend, however, is away from Western-style dress formalities creating an altogether more colourful and relaxed scene; black parliamentarians have adopted brightly-coloured African-style dress in place of the lacklustre grey suits of their predecessors. In seaside resorts beach culture permeates the business scene, and shorts and T-shirts are becoming the favoured garb.

Ndebele Art

*T*heir extraordinary art is the single aspect of South Ndebele culture that distinguishes it from that of other Nguni groups, such as the North Ndebele.

These stylish flowerpots are examples of the highly accomplished art of the Ndebele

Usually referred to simply as Ndebele, the South Ndebele live for the most part in the Eastern Transvaal Highveld, northeast of Pretoria. From house-painting to beadwork, mural-painting to the elaborate traditional dress style of the women, the Ndebele's striking attention to colour and pattern and their sense of symmetry are unusual.

In particular, the vibrant and colourful homesteads of the Transvaal rural landscape are a startling contrast to the typical earth-coloured dwellings around them. Although their decorative artistic tradition is an old one, in the past it was nothing like as ebullient as it became in the 1950s after the government stumbled on the idea of turning an Ndebele village near Pretoria into a showcase for tourists.

The palette of the original Ndebele house-painters was restricted to ochres, natural clays and charcoals. But in the '50s the government gave the women paints chosen from colour charts. A brighter, more elaborate style emerged and Ndebele art flourished; the examples we see around us today evolved as a result of this state patronage. The sinister side of the process was that it enabled the government to 'sell' ethnic identity, and to some extent helped underwrite apartheid and justify enforced relocation of indigenous groups into notional 'homelands'.

Despite this unfortunate history, Ndebele art and craft have extraordinary vitality. Painted houses, richly ornamented dress and ceremonial beadwork, like language and custom, proudly proclaim ethnic identity. But will this culture survive in the New South Africa? The attractions of the modern world are open to all, in theory anyway. Can labour-intensive artistic traditions such as the Ndebele's keep up the pace? Only time will tell.

WHAT TO SEE

'Faith can move mountains.
Faith can re-create a nation.'
HER MAJESTY THE QUEEN,
Cape Town, 1995

Western and Eastern Cape

*T*hree national highways leave Cape Town in the Western Cape and head into the heartland of South Africa. These arteries bravely traverse a phenomenal climatic, geographic and scenic range, and much of the landscape they pass through is a microcosm of the rest of the country.

One of these routes, the N1, is the start of a grandiose highway once destined to link Cape Town with Cairo. It skirts historic Cape Dutch Stellenbosch, shoots through the lush wine- and fruit-growing Breede River and Hex River Valleys, then enters the magnificent arid Karoo,

peppered with flat-topped *koppies* (rocky hillocks). It rushes on through the Free State to Johannesburg and Pretoria, and finally crosses the Limpopo River into Zimbabwe.

Namibia is linked to Cape Town by the N7. This route runs parallel to the

WESTERN AND EASTERN CAPE

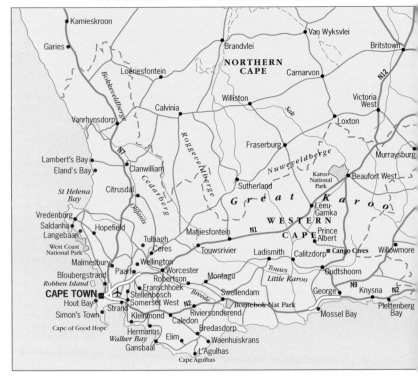

West Coast, skirts the rugged Cedarberg Mountains, and passes through the Olifants River Valley, where in the past elephants roamed. Today, in the spring, this desert route comes alive with millions of wild flowers. On it goes through the arid Northern Cape to the Orange River frontier.

A third national artery, the N2, skirts the southwestern seaboard, linking Cape Town to its summer riviera at Hermanus on Walker Bay. It passes a coast which, fringed by spotless white beaches, is wetted by a treacherous ocean which nonetheless provides excellent sport for sailors, surfers and swimmers. It bypasses Cape Agulhas at Africa's tip and, in the shadow of awe-inspiring mountain peaks, heads on to George, Knysna and Plettenberg Bay. This section of the N2, known as the Garden Route, runs parallel to the Outeniqua and Tsitsikamma Mountains and a coastline which features lakes, beaches, cliffs and ancient indigenous forests – a landscape of incomparable beauty. The N2 rambles on into the Eastern Cape and heads for Port Elizabeth after which it enters settler country, the Xhosa homelands, and Grahamstown.

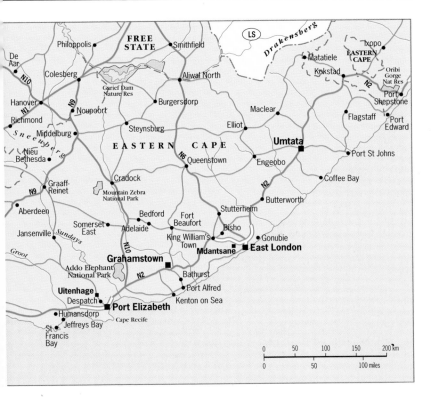

Cape Town

*I*n the 17th century Commander Jan van Riebeeck of the Dutch East India Company founded a settlement in the lap of flat-topped Table Mountain. This was to become South Africa's Mother City.

Today it is a place of immense contrasts, brash, yet at the same time highly cultured. Though hugely rich, with plush suburbs abutting the city centre, Cape Town also has some of South Africa's most dreadful townships in which poverty is endemic. Buffeted by mighty winds and deluged by torrential rains, yet with an incomparable fringe of beaches. Cape Town is perfection and imperfection in equal measure.

South Africa's oldest city has all the trappings of a civilised older world – gracious buildings, formal gardens, museums, art galleries and a wealth of tradition. It gave South Africa its Coloured population and Cape Dutch architecture. Here the Afrikaans language was born, and here the architect of apartheid, Dr Hendrik Verwoerd, was assassinated. Nelson Mandela was imprisoned for a considerable part of his adult life on Robben Island, just 9km off the city's shore. And it was in Cape Town on his release that he proclaimed freedom for the blacks.

There is plenty to do in and around this extraordinary city: it offers lively beach resorts; it is the hub of a beautiful mountainous peninsula with villages and beaches, walks and drives; and not 20 minutes from the city centre picnickers can find total solitude in one of the world's most important floral kingdoms.

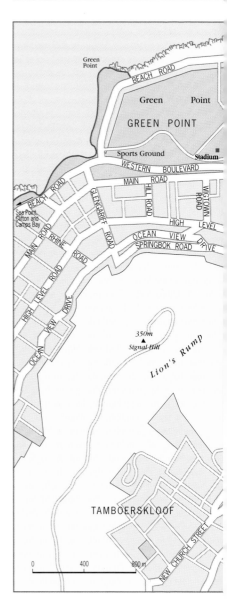

CAPE TOWN

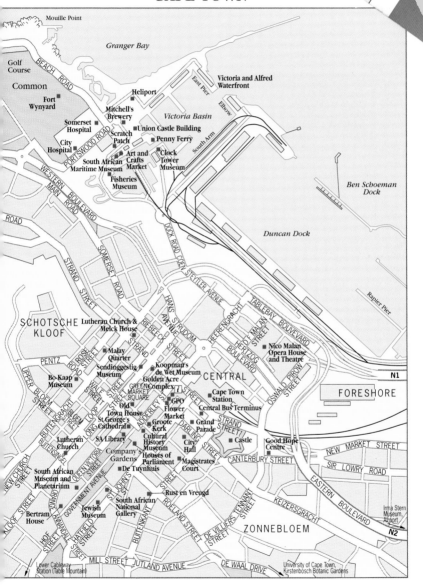

Mouille Point

Granger Bay

Golf
Course

Common

BEACH ROAD

Fort
Wynyard

Heliport

Mitchell's
Brewery

Somerset
Hospital

City
Hospital

PORTSWOOD ROAD

Scratch
Patch

South African
Maritime Museum

Fisheries
Museum

East Pier

Victoria and Alfred
Waterfront

Victoria Basin

Union Castle Building

Penny Ferry

Art and
Crafts
Market

Clock
Tower
Museum

Elbow

South Arm

Ben Schoeman
Dock

Duncan Dock

Rapier Pier

WESTERN BOULEVARD

MAIN ROAD

ROAD

STRAND STREET

SOMERSET ROAD

DOCK ROAD

COEN STEYTLER AVENUE

HANS STRIDOM

RIEBEECK STREET

STRAND

BUITENGRACHT

HERTZOG BOULEVARD

TABLEBAY BOULEVARD

D.F. MALAN STREET

SCHOTSCHE
KLOOF

Lutheran Church &
Melck House

PENTZ

ROSE STREET

LONG STREET

BREE STREET

Malay
Quarter

Sendinggestig
Museum

UPPER BLOEM STREET

Bo-Kaap
Museum

BUITENGRACHT

Koopman's
de Wet Museum

Golden Acre
Complex

GREEN
MARKET
SQUARE

Old
Town House

St George's
Cathedral

CENTRAL

Nico Malan
Opera House
and Theatre

OSWALD PIROW STREET

N1

Cape Town
Station

Central Bus Terminus

FORESHORE

LOOP STREET

WALE STREET

CASTLE STREET

ADDERLEY STREET

DARLING STREET

STRAND STREET

GPO

Flower
Market

Groote
Kerk

Grand
Parade

Castle

Good Hope
Centre

NEW MARKET STREET

Lutheran
Church

SA Library

BUITENSINGEL

Company's
Gardens

Cultural
History
Museum

Houses of
Parliament

De Tuynhuis

City
Hall

Magistrates
Court

CANTERBURY STREET

SIR LOWRY ROAD

EASTERN BOULEVARD

NEW CHURCH STREET

QUEEN VICTORIA STREET

GOVERNMENT AVENUE

South African
Museum and
Planetarium

Bertram
House

Jewish
Museum

Rust en Vreugd

South African
National Gallery

ST JOHN'S STREET

HOF STREET

ANNANDALE STREET

HATFIELD STREET

BUITENKANT STREET

ROELAND STREET

DE VILLIERS STREET

TENNANT STREET

KEIZERSGRACHT

ZONNEBLOEM

Irma Stern
Museum,
Airport

N2

KLOOF STREET

Lower Cableway
Station (Table Mountain)

MILL STREET   JUTLAND AVENUE

DE WAAL DRIVE

University of Cape Town,
Kirstenbosch Botanic Gardens

Kat Balcony, Castle of Good Hope. The original 'Kat' was a defensive wall

BERTRAM HOUSE

This late Georgian redbrick house is a typical example of early 19th-century Cape British domestic architecture. Within, the British Colonial House Museum illustrates the life-style of a well-to-do English family resident at the Cape.
Company's Gardens, top of Government Avenue. Tel: 021–24 9381. Open: Tuesday to Saturday 9.30am–4.30pm. Admission charge.

BO-KAAP AND MALAY QUARTER

The Bo-Kaap is a predominantly Muslim district where brightly painted late 18th- and early 19th-century houses are interspersed with mosques. Architecturally one of the country's most interesting areas, it suffered wilful destruction as a result of recent political ideology and decay. However, a particularly good survival houses the Bo-Kaap Museum whose exhibits detail the Islamic contribution to South Africa, Cape Malay cuisine and Afrikaans. Here

the first book in Afrikaans was written. The house is furnished as a typical home of a late 19th-century Muslim family.
Museum, 71 Wale Street. Tel: 021–24 3846. Open: Tuesday to Saturday 9.30am–4.30pm. Admission charge. For Bo-Kaap tours, call 021–24 0719.

CASTLE OF GOOD HOPE

Slaves built South Africa's oldest European building (begun 1666) using Robben Island stone and lime burnt from shells. Pentagonal in plan, it accords with the military concept that protruding corner bastions give better defence. At its heart, the famous baroque Kat Balcony, adorned with plaster reliefs by Anton Anreith (c1790), is one of the city's loveliest structures. Today the Castle is largely a museum housing the William Fehr Collection of Africana (see also Rust en Vreugd, page 45).
Castle Street. Tel: 021–400 1111. Open daily. Conducted tours hourly, 10am to 3pm. Admission charge.

CITY HALL AND GRAND PARADE

The City Hall (1905), with its clocktower and ponderous silhouette, is typical of town halls that dotted the Empire. Well restored, it is the seat of the Cape Town Symphony Orchestra. Concerts are held here on Thursdays and Sundays.

Facing it, the Grand Parade is the scene of weekly fleamarkets (Wednesdays and Saturdays), and daily flower sellers and taxi-drivers compete noisily for business. The Parade's political role, which it lost in the repression, was revived in 1990 when an estimated 100,000 people gathered here to hear Nelson Mandela speak minutes after his release from gaol. His first public address after 27 years in captivity began thus:

'Amandla! Iafrika! Mayibuye!' ('Power to the People!').
Darling Street. Tel: 021–461 7086.

COMPANY'S GARDEN

Fresh fruit and vegetables from the Dutch East India Company's garden were destined for ships plying the route between Europe and the East. Although only a fraction of the 17th-century's 18 hectares survive, today the garden is a welcome area of green in a busy city. It contains magnificent indigenous and exotic plants and a quiet café.
Top of Adderley Street.
Open: daily 7am to sunset.

GREEN MARKET SQUARE

The second-oldest square in the city is also one of Cape Town's most successful open spaces. Created in 1710 as a market, it contains the city's first civic building – the Old Town House (see page 45). It has always been a convivial meeting place, and today it is the scene of a lively fleamarket (daily – weather permitting).

Green Market Square, busy with the daily fleamarket

GROOTE KERK

In the Cape's earliest days church services were heard on Jan van Riebeeck's ship, the *Dromedaris*. Only in 1704 did the settlement acquire a proper venue for Dutch Reformed services – the thatch-roofed precursor of the present edifice (1841). The wooden pulpit, the work of Anton Anreith (1788), is still *in situ*. The Groote Kerk, the oldest church in the country (1704), is the mother church for the Dutch Reformed Church in South Africa.
Adderley Street. Tel: 021–461 7044. Open: weekdays 10am–2pm. For other Anreith works, see the Lutheran Church (page 45), and Groot Constantia (see page 48).

Koopman's de Wet House, an elegant jewel in an undistinguished setting

former home houses an excellent small collection of her work as well as a range of treasures she collected on her travels in Africa and abroad: rare Congolese items, Greek artefacts, Buddhist art and pre-Columbian masks.

The Firs, Cecil Road, Rosebank. Tel: 021–685 5686. Open: Tuesday to Sunday 10am–1pm, 2–5pm. Admission charge.

JEWISH MUSEUM

The first service in South Africa's oldest synagogue occurred on Yom Kippur, 1841. Now a museum, it contains items of religious and historical significance and traces the history of Jewish communities in the Cape.

84 Hatfield Street, Company's Gardens. Tel: 021–45 1546. Open: Tuesday and Thursday 2–5pm, Sunday 10am–2.30pm. Admission charge.

KOOPMAN'S DE WET HOUSE

That Koopman's de Wet House, built in 1701 in once-fashionable Strand Street, survived the developers is remarkable. Much altered, its large rooms are elaborately adorned with illusionistic paint effects, and there is a magnificent collection of Cape furniture and porcelain put together by the de Wet sisters whose family occupied the house for most of the 19th century and until it became a museum.

35 Strand Street. Tel: 021–24 2473. Open: Tuesday to Saturday 9.30am–4.30pm. Admission charge.

LONG STREET

From sea to mountain, Long Street is flanked by a riotous profusion of churches, mosques, shops, banks, offices,

HOUSES OF PARLIAMENT AND TUYNHUIS

Cape Town is the home of the country's legislature. The exterior of the brick and stucco Parliament building (1884), like the interior, is gloomy and old-fashioned. History is in the making here, and a visit to the public gallery during a parliamentary session will not go unrewarded. Next door, the Tuynhuis (built 1700, restored 1795), originally the Dutch East India Company's Guest House, is now the office of the state president.

Parliament Street and Government Avenue. Tel: 021–403 2911. Tickets available for parliamentary sessions (January to June) on presentation of passport. During the recess (July to January) guided tours weekends, 11am and 2pm. Enter via Parliament Street gate.

IRMA STERN MUSEUM

Irma Stern (1894–1966) is perhaps South Africa's best-known painter. Her

apartment blocks, cafés, restaurants and clubs. Here you can buy anything from books and beads to *boerewors* (sausage) and fine wine, lounge all day in a pub or shop for antiques. Its reputation is equally colourful, and its whores and drag queens, Chinese sailors and drinkers have a hallowed niche in the annals of maritime lore.

LUTHERAN CHURCH AND MELCK HOUSE

South Africa's first Lutheran church (built 1774) contains a magnificent wooden pulpit by Anton Anreith (1784), who also remodelled the entrance façade in 1791. Next door, Melck House, once the parsonage, is now a restaurant.
96 Strand Street. Open: weekdays 8.30am–1pm, 1.30–4.30pm.

OLD TOWN HOUSE

As the early settlement expanded, fire became an ever-present hazard and the streets needed patrolling nightly by a Watch. This was the Burgher Watch's

base and seat of the Burgher Council (begun 1755). Proclamations were read from the balcony to citizens summoned by the bell in the tower on the roof. Today the building houses a collection of 17th-century Dutch and Flemish paintings donated by Rand baron Max Michaelis.
Green Market Square. Tel: 021–24 6367. Open: daily 10am–5pm. Admission charge.

RUST EN VREUGD

The name of this fine 18th-century Cape house means 'rest and joy'. Formerly the home of the state prosecutor, today it contains part of the William Fehr Collection of Africana (see also Castle of Good Hope, page 42), watercolours, engravings and lithographs by early African artists.
78 Buitenkant Street. Tel: 021–45 3628. Open: weekdays 9.30am–4pm. Admission charge.

Rust en Vreugd, once the home of the state prosecutor, now houses a museum

SOUTH AFRICAN CULTURAL HISTORY MUSEUM

Slaves, first brought to the Cape in 1685, were housed here for 130 years. In 1811 it was converted into government offices and today it is a museum dedicated to the study of the country's various population groups, with displays of coins, weapons, furniture, ceramics, stamps and textiles.

49 Adderley Street. Tel: 021–461 8280. Open: Monday to Saturday 9.30am–4.30pm. Admission charge.

SOUTH AFRICAN LIBRARY

One of the world's first free libraries (founded 1818), this national reference and preservation library is the oldest cultural institution in South Africa. There are regular exhibitions based on its rich collections.

Queen Victoria Street. Tel: 021–24 6320. Open: weekdays 9am–6pm, Saturday 9am–1pm.

SOUTH AFRICAN MUSEUM AND PLANETARIUM

The country's oldest museum (1825) is dedicated to the natural sciences and anthropology. From replica dinosaurs to examples of San rock art, there is much to see. The Planetarium is the best place to begin an exploration of the Southern hemisphere's night sky.

25 Queen Victoria Street. Tel: 021–24 3330. Open: daily 10am–5pm. Admission charge (free on Wednesday).

SOUTH AFRICAN NATIONAL GALLERY

The gallery has a fine international art collection and a comprehensive collection of contemporary South African art. Alongside works from the past, is the art of experimentation and 'township art', tribal and ethnic art (Ndebele, Fingo, Xhosa, Zulu beadwork). There are also excellent changing exhibitions.

Government Avenue, Company's Gardens. Tel: 021–45 1628. Open: daily Monday 1–5pm, Tuesday to Sunday 10am–5pm. Free.

ST GEORGE'S CATHEDRAL

The Anglican cathedral of Archbishop Desmond Tutu was begun in 1901 to the

Old and new: South Africa Museum (1825) and the Planetarium (1987)

Take a cable-car trip up Table Mountain for spectacular views

designs of Herbert Baker. Its Gothic Revival character is more English than African, and it comes complete with stained-glass windows dedicated to Lord Mountbatten. Tutu's sermons are always worth hearing.
Wale Street.

TABLE MOUNTAIN AND CABLEWAY

Table Mountain provides Cape Town with its unique setting, making it one of the world's most beautiful cities. It forms the bold northern front of a high range stretching 50km to Cape Point. Flanked by Lion's Head and Signal Hill (right) and Devil's Peak (left), its elevation is 1,086m, of which 500m is a vertical face of bare, layered sandstone. Gulleys, ravines and slopes provide almost unlimited possibilities for walking and climbing, while a cable car transports passengers to the summit's viewing platforms and restaurant.
The cableway operates daily, weather permitting. Open: November 8am–9.30pm,

December to mid-January 7am–10.30pm, end of January to end of April 8am–9.30pm, May to October 8.30am–5.30pm. Tickets bookable in advance from Waterfront Information Centre, tel: 021–418 2369, and Lower Cable Station, tel: 021–24 5148. Admission charge.

VICTORIA AND ALFRED WATERFRONT

For decades city and sea have been separated by the Foreshore, an ugly, reclaimed area straddled by flyovers and parking lots. But now, in a highly acclaimed regeneration project, the atmospheric old harbour area is bustling with shops, restaurants, bars, cinemas, markets, a hotel and museums, while retaining its prime function as an active harbour.
Victoria and Alfred Basins, Table Bay Harbour. Tel: 021–418 2369.

Cape Town Environs

GROOT CONSTANTIA MANOR HOUSE AND WINE MUSEUM

Wines from this Constantia estate once kept Napoleon happy in exile. They are still produced here today (see pages 170–1) and can be tasted. Apart from its incomparable setting in the shade of magnificent old oaks, the estate's Cape Dutch manor house (built in 1685 and subsequently much restored), is one of the Cape's grandest. Built by Governor Simon van der Stel, it is now a museum of early Cape furniture, paintings, and Delft and Rhenish earthenware. The estate has an excellent wine museum in the old wine cellars, two restaurants, a shop and tours of the modern wine-making operations.

About 15km south of the city centre. Take the M3 to the Constantia exit. Museum – tel: 021–794 5067. Open: daily 10am–5pm. Admission charge.

Carved pediment at Groot Constantia Manor, a superb example of Cape Dutch architecture

KIRSTENBOSCH BOTANIC GARDENS

In 1913 the National Botanical Gardens were founded, their site part of the estate Cecil Rhodes bought in 1895 as a way of preserving the eastern flank of Table Mountain, and which he bequeathed to the nation. Devoted almost exclusively to the indigenous flora of southern Africa, it contains about 9,000 of South Africa's 22,000 plant species. Plants selected for inclusion have horticultural potential, are of botanical interest, enjoy rare and endangered status, or are used for educational or scientific purposes. Through careful selection there are displays of flowers throughout the year even though native plants are very seasonal in nature. There are walks, a popular restaurant open for breakfast, lunch and tea, and a garden shop selling plants and flora-related books.

About 10km south of the city centre. Rhodes Drive, Newlands. Tel: 021–761 4916. Open: daily, April to August 8am–6pm;

*September to March 8am–7pm. Admission
charge. Guided walks – Tuesday and
Saturday. Call the Flowerline for
information about where the best spring wild
flowers are to be seen that day. Tel:
021–418 3705.*

ROBBEN ISLAND
This tiny island of banishment is the
most symbolically charged piece of land
in South Africa. Its name derives from
'*robbe*', the Dutch word for seals. Since
the 17th century political prisoners and
criminals were dumped here, and in the
19th century it was home to various
African leaders who had attempted to
resist the advance of the colonial frontier.
In the 1960s victims of state oppression
were detained on the island, most
famously Nelson Mandela. The island
has been called the University of the
Struggle – incarcerated here, some of
South Africa's finest political minds
helped to educate their fellow prisoners.
Even the guards had to be replaced
regularly as they discovered the difficulty
of defending apartheid in the company of
rational, intelligent men.
*9km north, off the Green Point coast. Half-
day trips on Tuesday, Wednesday and
Saturday on application to the Commander,
Public Relations, PB Robben Island 7400.
Tel: 021–411 1006.*

RONDEVLEI BIRD SANCTUARY
Located on the edge of the Cape Flats,
this nature reserve is a sanctuary for over
200 species of Cape bird. It is also home
to a small herd of hippo at nearby
Zeekoeivlei ('hippo lake'), a reminder of
how prolific this beast once was around
Cape Town. There are waterside hides
for watching the hippo, and observation
towers for birdwatching.
Cape Flats, about 22km south of the city

Kirstenbosch Botanic Gardens, near Constantia,
in their dramatic setting

*centre. Perth Road, Grassy Park. Tel:
021–706 2404. Open: daily 8am–5pm.
Admission charge.*

WORLD OF BIRDS SANCTUARY
This is one of the largest bird sanctuaries
in South Africa. Over 450 varieties (there
are more than 3,000 birds) are housed in
walk-through aviaries designed to
simulate natural habitats.
*About 25km southwest of the city centre.
Valley Road, Hout Bay. Tel: 021–790
2730. Open: daily 9am–6pm. Admission
charge.*

FLORA

Nearly 10 per cent of all the flowering plants on Earth, are found in a variety of different terrains dotted about South Africa. This is the country in which many of the world's favourite garden plants, such as arum lilies, chinkerinchees, gladioli and freesias, have their origins.

No region is more prolifically endowed than the Western Cape. Here *fynbos* ('fine bush' – a natural heathland type of vegetation characterised by its range of ericas) occurs along a narrow belt stretching north and east of Cape Town. Most famous for its proteas, of which one, the king protea, is South Africa's national flower, this small area hosts over 7,300 species of plants. An astonishing 5,000 of these occur nowhere else in the world, and the Cape Peninsula, home to the Cape of Good Hope Nature Reserve and the Kirstenbosch National Botanical Gardens, is guardian of a substantial portion. *Fynbos* is also the major vegetation type of the Cape Floral Kingdom, the smallest and, for its size, the richest of the world's six floral kingdoms.

The flora of the Eastern Cape is also rich

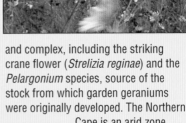

and complex, including the striking crane flower (*Strelizia reginae*) and the *Pelargonium* species, source of the stock from which garden geraniums were originally developed. The Northern Cape is an arid zone with an extraordinary range of succulents, some of which have adapted to unpredictable amounts of rain and hot summers. By contrast, the coast of KwaZulu/Natal enjoys a tropical climate and has a vegetation to match. It

The edible fruit of the baobab, one of the largest of all tropical trees

Drakensberg flora (above)
Protea (right); bloom of the Kaffirboom (below right)

may not be as rich as the Cape, but the flora of the Drakensberg is studded with attractive flowering plants adapted to the short, cool summers and the cold winters.

Moving inland, on to the plateau of the Highveld, grassland and its associated flora merge into bushveld and, in the far north, beyond the Soutpansberg Mountains, becomes open woodland, a key feature of which is the remarkable baobab tree with its enormous trunk.

Precious survivors of the great elephant herds that once roamed the Addo

ADDO ELEPHANT NATIONAL PARK

By 1931 the Eastern Cape was down to its last 11 elephants. Huge herds once roamed across this region but, following its development for farming early this century, most elephants were eradicated. The survivors were nurtured in this 11,718-hectare reserve and today around 170 beasts (reputed to be the most aggressive in Africa) are found here. Their protection has helped to preserve a unique ecosystem which supports a variety of other creatures. The park has a rest camp with chalets, caravan and camp sites, a restaurant and a shop. There are two walking trails, one including a hide overlooking a waterhole in the Addo bush.

60km north of Port Elizabeth, on the R335. National Parks Board, PO Box 787, Pretoria 0001. Tel: 012–343 1991. Open: all year round.

BREEDE RIVER VALLEY

Trout fishermen, nature lovers and mountaineers will all enjoy the Breede River Valley in the southwestern Cape, an important fruit and wine producing area. Around Ceres you can pick fruit or buy fruit juice and dried or fresh fruit. Worcester, the 'capital', is the country's biggest wine-producing district and keeper of the vast KWV brandy cellars. It also has the Kleinplasie Open Air Museum illustrating the lifestyle of pioneer farmers. Near by, the Karoo National Botanical Garden contains 144 hectares of natural semi-desert vegetation, 10 hectares of landscaped gardens featuring astonishing plants from the country's drier parts, and a world-famous collection of stone plants. In Montagu there is an interesting museum of local history and a popular hot mineral spa (35.5°C) – the Montagu Spring.

Ceres is about 158km northeast of Cape Town, Worcester is about 105km northeast of Cape Town, and Montagu is about 280km east of Cape Town. Breede River Valley Tourist Information, PO Box 91, Worcester 6850. Tel: 0231–70945. Kleinplasie Open Air Museum, PO Box 557, Worcester 6849. Tel: 0231–22225. Open: Monday to Saturday 9am–4.30pm, Sunday 10.30am–4.30pm. Admission charge. Karoo National Botanical Garden. Tel: 0231–70785. Open: August to October, Monday to Sunday 10am–4pm. Montagu Museum, Long Street. Tel: 0234–41950. Open: weekdays 9am–1pm, 2–5pm, weekends 10am–noon. Admission charge.

CAPE AGULHAS AND AROUND

Two hours from Cape Town is Cape Agulhas, Africa's southernmost tip, where the Indian and Atlantic Oceans meet, washing a coast of wide, sandy beaches, cliffs, caves and coves. The sea here is murderous; what Rudyard Kipling called the 'dread Agulhas roll' drowned many a seaman, and graves and wrecks litter the coast. The Shipwreck Museum at Bredasdorp, gateway to this area, reveals the details, displaying salvaged figureheads, coins and shipboard furniture from stricken vessels.

A wreck of 1815 gave its name to Arniston (also called Waenhuiskrans – 'wagon house cliff' – after an enormous nearby cave), a seaside village famous for its 19th-century fishermen's cottages. Going west, L'Agulhas at Cape Agulhas is one of a series of small beach resorts where the angling is excellent, and Elim is an historic Moravian mission village with one of the finest early streetscapes in the Cape. Northeast of Bredasdorp, 36,000-hectare De Hoop Nature Reserve, important for the conservation of rare lowland *fynbos*, is home to various animals including the rare Cape mountain zebra. The birdlife is prolific. This reserve has accommodation, hiking trails, walks and drives.

Cape Agulhas is about 220km southeast of Cape Town. Agulhas Publicity Association. Tel: 02846–620. Bredasdorp Shipwreck Museum, Independent Street. Tel: 02481–41240. Open: weekdays 9am–4.45pm, Saturday 9am–2.45pm, Sunday 10.30am–12.30pm. Admission charge. De Hoop Nature Reserve, Private Bag X16, 7280 Bredasdorp. Tel: 02922–782.

Fishing boats at Arniston. This peaceful scene belies a sometimes treacherous sea

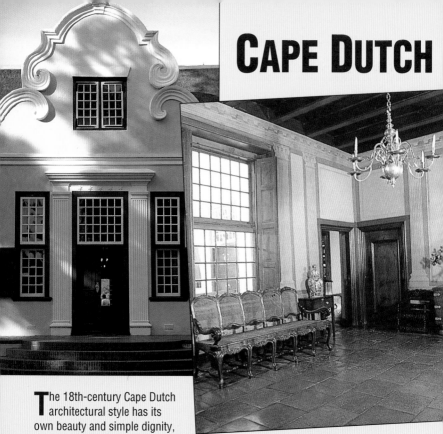

CAPE DUTCH

The 18th-century Cape Dutch architectural style has its own beauty and simple dignity, the Cape Dutch farmhouses being particularly impressive in their formal grouping with surrounding farm buildings. Uniquely South African, the style is a distinct regional type, created in response to local circumstances as well as wider aspirations and more distant influences.

The most characteristic feature is the distinctive gable over the main entrance. Recognisable from afar, the flamboyant gable design probably derives from the baroque architecture of the northern Netherlands. It was intended as a show of status; on houses of consequence, gables were often very richly decorated with fine plasterwork and the building's date.

The Cape Dutch farmhouse formula is simple: a single storey, based on the H-, T- or U-plan and built of sun-baked brick with a reed-thatched roof. Exterior walls were plastered with clay and whitewashed, and room sizes were determined by the lengths of beams available from local forests or the nearest shipwreck. In front of the main door is a raised *stoep,* or terrace, of brick.

The earliest houses were simple rectangles: one room led into another

ARCHITECTURE

Above – from left to right:
Vergelegen Manor House,
Koopman's de Wet House,
Groot Constantia
Left: detail at Groot Constantia

gave on to the rest of the house. Some interiors were merely whitewashed while others were decorated with *trompe l'oeil* wall paintings. Interior beauty and character comes mainly from with the kitchen at the far end. Later, as plans became more elaborate, the entrance door led into the *voorkamer* (front room), separated from the *agterkamer* (back room) by a decorative wooden screen. From these centrally placed rooms, doors ceilings and floors which were made of massive beams and planks of yellow wood, and from panelled doors of similar material with stinkwood surrounds. In some houses, floors were of polished red Batavian tiles.

Vineyards are a feature of the lovely valley around Franschhoek

CEDARBERG MOUNTAINS

The vast Cedarberg range takes its name from *Widdringtonia cedarbergensis*, a species of cedar which grows at 1,000 to 1,500m. Extending north-south for about 100km, the Cedarberg provides wonderful hiking. See the entire range – with its bizarre sandstone formations, clear pools and caves with San rock paintings – on a two-week trip by donkey. The Algeria forestry station has an excellent camp site; Clanwilliam and Citrusdal both have hotels.

The Cedarberg is about 220km north of Cape Town. For hiking permits and information, Cedarberg Wilderness Area, Private Bag X1, Citrusdal 7340. Tel: 02682–3440. Olifants River Valley Tourist Information, PO Box 5, Clanwilliam 8135. Tel: 027–482 2029.

EAST LONDON AND AROUND

East London beaches, Nahoon Beach in particular, have some of the best surfing in the country. East London Museum contains the world's only dodo egg and a stuffed coelacanth (see page 23). Visit Gately House Museum for a good small collection of Cape furniture, and the Anne Bryant Art Gallery for contemporary South African art. Nearby King William's Town was an important military base in the 19th century. Here, the Kaffrarian Museum has a large natural history section, and excellent displays of Xhosa culture in its Xhosa Museum annexe.

East London is about 60km west of King William's Town. East London tourist information, Old Library Building, Argyle Street. Museum, Oxford Street. Tel: 0431–26015. Open: weekdays 9.30am–5pm, Saturday 9.30am–noon, Sunday 11am–4pm. Admission charge. Gately House Museum, Queen Street. Tel: 0431–22141. Open: weekends only, 3–5pm. Anne Bryant Art Gallery, between St Mark's and St Luke's Road. Tel: 0431–342209. Open: weekdays 9am–5pm,

Saturday 9.30am–noon. Kaffrarian Museum, Main Street. Tel: 0433–24506. Open: weekdays 9am–12.45pm, 2–5pm.

FRANSCHHOEK
Here, Governor Simon van der Stel granted land (1688) to Huguenot refugees from France, remembered in the names of the farms in 'French Corner' – and the French surnames of many of today's Afrikaans-speaking owners. There is a Huguenot Museum, adjacent to the modern Huguenot Memorial. Franschhoek is a wine-growing district, and many of the estates, dominated by spectacular Cape Dutch manors can be visited.

Franschhoek is about 80km east of Cape Town. Huguenot Museum and tourist information, Lambrecht Street. Tel: 02212–2532. Open: Monday to Saturday 9am–1pm, 2–5pm; Sunday 2–5pm. Admission charge.

GRAHAMSTOWN
Originally a military outpost (1812) on the eastern frontier of the Cape Colony, Grahamstown grew following the arrival of British settlers in 1820. Today it is an important cultural and educational centre dominated by Rhodes University. At the Albany Museum (founded in 1855), you can learn about Xhosa traditions and the history of the 1820 Settlers, and in its Observatory Museum annexe find out about South Africa's diamond industry. If fish are your passion, visit the J L B Smith Institute of Ichthyology. The Natural History Museum is concerned with displays on early humans in South Africa.

Grahamstown is 130km northeast of Port Elizabeth. Grahamstown Publicity Association, Church Square. Tel: 0461–23241. Albany Museum, Somerset Street. Open: weekdays 9.30am–1pm, 2–5pm, weekends 2–5pm. Observatory Museum, Bathurst Street. Open: weekdays 9.30am–1pm, 2–5pm; Saturday 9am–1pm. J L B Smith Institute of Ichthyology, Somerset Street. Open: weekdays 8.30am–1pm, 2–5pm. Natural History Museum, Somerset Street. Open: weekdays 9.30am–1pm, 2–5pm; Saturday 2–5pm. Tel: 0461–22312 for museums listed above; admission charge for each.

Ornate architecture graces the old settler capital of Grahamstown

Peace and quiet at Hermanus: collecting white mussels on the beach

Karoo National Park. Before the introduction of sheep by pioneers, hundreds of thousands of springbok used to migrate across its plains. Springbok still flourish here today. Near by, Beaufort West is a pleasant stop-over on the Cape Town–Johannesburg route. Graaff-Reinet, founded in 1786, has over 200 buildings designated National Monuments.

The Owl House at Nieu Bethesda (about 60km from Graaff-Reinet) is a monument to the eccentric sculptor Helen Martins, and is the subject of annual pilgrimage by her admirers. Her work – sculptures of owls and strangely naïve-style human figures – fills the garden.
Graaff-Reinet is about 748km northeast of Cape Town. Central Karoo Tourist Information, PO Box 56, Beaufort West 6970. Tel: 0201–51160. Karoo National Park, National Parks Board. Tel: 012–343 1991. Karoo Nature Reserve, PO Box 349, Graaff-Reinet 6280. Tel: 0491–23453.

LITTLE KAROO

The approach to the area via Prince Albert and the 24km-long Swartberg Pass is a spectacular mountain route. Beyond, the awesome Cango Caves are three huge sequences of caves adorned with fantastic dripstone formations.
The Cango Caves are 29km north of Oudtshoorn. Open: 364 days a year, 8am–5pm. Tours conducted daily. Tel: 0443–227410. Klein Karoo Tourist Information, PO Box 1234, Oudtshoorn 6620. Tel: 0443–226643.

MATJIESFONTEIN

The 19th-century resort of Matjiesfontein is popular with weekenders from Cape Town. The restored Lord Milner Hotel,

HERMANUS

Focused on its Old Harbour and museum, the fashionable summer resort of Hermanus is a place to relax, play sport – or whale-watch: the southern right whales migrate to Walker Bay between June and November to calve. Not far away is the Harold Porter Nature Reserve, an important botanical garden.
Hermanus is 100km southeast of Cape Town on the scenic R44. Hermanus Publicity Association, PO Box 117, Hermanus 7200. Tel: 0283–22629. Old Harbour Museum, Marine Drive. Tel: 0283–21475. Open: weekdays 9am–1pm, 2–4pm; Saturday 9am–1pm. Free. Harold Porter Nature Reserve. Tel: 02823–9711. Open: daily 8am–4pm.

GREAT KAROO

To see the Great Karoo in its virgin state, visit the spectacular 32,000-hectare

first opened in 1884, is a monument to Victorian standards of comfort.

Matjiesfontein is about 260km northeast of Cape Town.

MOUNTAIN ZEBRA NATIONAL PARK

This 6,536-hectare reserve, a sanctuary for the orange-muzzled Cape mountain zebra, has excellent nature trails and walks. Accommodation varies from reasonably comfortable to spartan, and there is a restaurant and shop. Nearby Cradock was the childhood home of Olive Schreiner, author of *The Story of an African Farm* (1883).

The park is about 20km west of Cradock, which is 240km from Port Elizabeth. National Parks Board. Tel: 012–343 1991. Olive Schreiner Museum, corner of Kruis and Bree streets, PO Box 638, Cradock 5880. Tel: 0431–5251. Open: Thursday to Tuesday 8am–12.45pm, 2–4pm. Admission charge.

PORT ELIZABETH AND AROUND

Port Elizabeth dates from 1820, when 4,000 British settlers arrived. Its evolution as an important port gained it the title of 'the Liverpool of the Cape Colony'. Now South Africa's fifth city, it has plenty for visitors: beaches, good shops and restaurants, museums and galleries – including the Port Elizabeth Museum, the Castle Hill Historical Museum and the King George VI Art Gallery – as well as a Snake Park and Tropical House, and an Oceanarium.

Port Elizabeth is 769km east of Cape Town. Port Elizabeth Tourist Information, Pleinhuis, Market Square. Tel: 041–52 1315. Port Elizabeth Museum, Beach Road, Humewood. Tel: 041–56 1051. Open: daily 9am–1pm, 2–5pm. Castle Hill Historical Museum, 7 Castle Hill. Tel: 041–52 2515. Open: Monday and Sunday 2–5pm, Tuesday to Saturday 10am–1pm, 2–5pm. King George VI Art Gallery, Park Drive. Tel: 041–56 1030. Open: weekdays 8.30am–5pm, Saturday 8.30am–4.30pm, Sunday 2–4.30pm. Snake Park, Tropical House and Oceanarium, Beach Road, Humewood. Tel: 041–56 1051. Open: daily 9am–1pm, 2–5pm. Admission charge for all of the above.

The impressive stalactites and stalagmites of Cango Caves, near Oudtshoorn

Ostrich farms still exist around Oudtshoorn, once 'feather capital' of the world

OUDTSHOORN

Oudtshoorn (founded 1843) grew rich on ostrich feathers, and once had more millionaires than anywhere else. The Dorpshuis, a magnate's 'ostrich feather palace', is now a museum and you can trace the town's history at the C P Nel Museum. At Highgate, one of the original ostrich farms, you can watch them race, buy their eggs or eat them. The Safari Ostrich Farm has a restored feather baron's mansion, the eccentric Welgeluk (1910).

506km east of Cape Town. Publicity Association, corner of Baron van Rheede and Voortrekker streets. Tel: 0443–222221. Dorpshuis, 146 High Street. Tel: 0443–223676. C P Nel Museum, Baron van Rheede Street. Tel: 0443–227306. Open: Monday to Saturday 8.30am–1pm, 2–5pm. Admission charge. Highgate Ostrich Farm, PO Box 94, Oudtshoorn 6620. Tel: 0443–227115. Safari Ostrich Farm, PO Box 300 Oudtshoorn 6620. Tel: 0443–227311.

STELLENBOSCH

South Africa's second oldest town, home to the Afrikaans Stellenbosch University,

has retained much of its early character. The Village Museum incorporates four period houses illustrating architectural development between 1709 and 1929. The best way to explore town is on foot.

Stellenbosch is the start of the Stellenbosch Wine Route (see page169) – visit it in conjunction with the Stellenryck Wine Museum and the Oude Meester Brandy Museum.

Stellenbosch is 48km east of Cape Town. Tourist Information, 30 Plein Street, Stellenbosch 7600. Tel: 02231–833584. Village Museum, Ryneveld Street. Tel: 02231–72902. Open: Monday to Saturday 9.30am–5pm, Sunday 2–5pm. Admission charge. Stellenryck Wine Museum, Dorp Street. Tel: 02231–73480. Open: weekdays 9am–12.45pm, 2–5pm; Saturday 10am–1pm, 2–5pm; Sunday 2.30–5.30pm. Admission charge. Oude Meester Brandy Museum, Old Strand Road. Open: weekdays 9am–12.15pm, 2–5pm; Saturday 10am–1pm, 2–5pm; Sunday 2.30–5pm. Admission charge. Stellenbosch Historical Walks. Tel: 021–883-9633. (NB – some numbers in Stellenbosch will be prefixed with 88 – contact the operator if you have difficulty.)

SWELLENDAM AND AROUND

Swellendam's Drostdy (1747), the regional seat of colonial authority and one of the finest such buildings in the country, is now the focus of a museum complex. To Swellendam's south, the 2,740-hectare Bontebok National Park has a thriving herd of the rare bontebok, once facing extinction.

Swellendam is 215km east of Cape Town. Tourist Information, 36 Voortrekker Street. Tel: 0291–42770. Museum complex, 18 Swellengrebel Street. Tel: 0291–41138. Open: weekdays 9am–4.45pm, Saturday 10am–4pm. Bontebok National Park. Tel: 0291–42735. Admission charge.

TULBAGH

Destroyed by an earthquake in1969, Tulbagh was restored and today is an almost perfect image of an 18th-century South African rural town. The rebuilt Drostdy is now a museum, and the Oude Kerk Volksmuseum (Old Church Folk Museum), a complex of restored buildings, exhibits furniture and costumes.

160km northeast of Cape Town. Tulbagh Publicity Association. Tel: 0236–301348.

Oude Kerk Volksmuseum, 4 Church Street. Tel: 0236–301041. Open: weekdays 9am–1pm, 2–5pm. Sunday 11am–12.30pm, 2–4.30pm. Admission charge. Oude Drostdy Museum, 4km outside town on Van der Stel Street. Tel: 02362–203. Open: Monday to Saturday 10am–1pm, 2–5pm. Admission charge.

WEST COAST

The West Coast's main resort, lagoonside Langebaan, is near the 20,000-hectare West Coast National Park, wetlands protecting thousands of wading birds that summer in South Africa. Offshore islands offer predator-proof nesting sites for an estimated three-quarters of a million seabirds. Further up the coast Saldanha Bay is a huge natural harbour famous for its mussels. St Helena Bay and Elands Bay are both good for surfing.

West Coast National Park is 122km north of Cape Town. National Parks Board. Tel: 012–343 1991. West Coast Tourist Information, PO Box 139, Saldanha, 7395. Tel: 02281–42058.

Start your walk around Stellenbosch among the historic buildings of Dorp Street

The Cape Peninsula

The Cape Peninsula's mountain chain curves south from Cape Town, dips at Constantia Nek, rises at the Constantiaberg, falls away over Silvermine to the Fish Hoek Valley, then swings past Simon's Town to the southeast. For 12km, before finally tumbling into the sea at Cape Point, it blends into the unspoiled wilderness of the Cape of Good Hope Nature Reserve. *Allow one day.*

In the centre of Cape Town, take Somerset Road at its junction with Buitengracht Street and continue along Main Road through Sea Point to the M6.

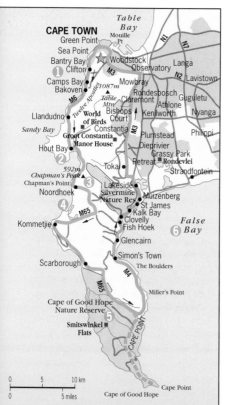

1 THE ATLANTIC SEABOARD

Sea Point's Promenade is a favourite stretch for slow walks. Further on, at Bantry Bay, little Saunders Rock beach with its tidal pool offers safe bathing. Beyond, Clifton has the country's most fashionable beaches. Next door, Camps Bay's beaches are sprawled dramatically at the foot of the magnificent Twelve Apostles. The road winds on past Bakoven to Llandudno, picturesquely climbing up steep slopes, and Sandy Bay, a nudist beach.

The M6 climbs the hill above Llandudno, then descends towards Hout Bay.

2 HOUT BAY

Wood (*hout*) was obtained here for early Cape Town buildings. The village has a beach and a fishing harbour and is the centre of the snoek industry and base of the crayfishing fleet. The World of Birds Sanctuary (see page 49) is in the Hout Bay Valley.

Return to the M6 and follow the signs to Chapman's Peak.

3 CHAPMAN'S PEAK

The 10km drive around Chapman's Peak to Noordhoek is one of the world's most spectacular scenic passes, with exceptional views across the bay. It gives access to excellent climbs and mountain walks.
From Noordhoek, follow the M6 from which, after the first lights, the M65 branches right to Kommetjie.

4 NOORDHOEK AND KOMMETJIE

Noordhoek's lovely 6km Long Beach is favoured by horseback riders. At its end, Kommetjie is a quiet village with a popular surfing beach. A shallow tidal pool provides safe bathing for children.
From Kommetjie, the M65 continues through Scarborough to the Cape of Good Hope Nature Reserve.

5 CAPE OF GOOD HOPE NATURE RESERVE

This magnificent 7,750-hectare nature reserve (mountain zebra, bontebok, eland, baboons) straddles the peninsula's tip. There are drives and places to picnic and swim.
At the exit, turn right if you want to visit the southern tip, then return north, turning right on to the M4 to Simon's Town.

6 FALSE BAY

The approach to Simon's Town is via The Boulders, where the swimming, among huge boulders, is shared with a colony of jackass penguins. Simon's Town, South Africa's naval base, is a quaint seaside town beyond which Fish Hoek is a popular resort with wide, safe beaches. Kalk Bay, with antique, junk and craft shops, is home to the False Bay fishing fleet. Beyond, St James has a small beach with a tidal pool. Alongside it, Muizenberg's magnificent beach offers safe bathing. Visit the Natale Labia

Cape Point, where the Peninsula ends

Museum here, a satellite of the S A National Gallery, and Rhodes Cottage memorial museum.
Continue on the M4 past Lakeside, then left on to the M42 to pick up the M3 which leads back to the city.

Cape of Good Hope Nature Reserve. Tel: 021–780 1100. Open: daily. Admission charge.
Simon's Town Museum, Court Road. Tel: 021–786 3046. Open: Tuesday to Friday 9am–4pm, Saturday 10am–1pm.
Natale Labia Museum, Main Road, Muizenberg. Tel: 021–788 4106. Open: Tuesday to Sunday 10am–5pm, closed during August.
Rhodes Cottage, Main Road, Muizenberg. Tel: 021–788 1816. Open: Tuesday to Sunday 10am–1pm, 2–5pm.

The Garden Route

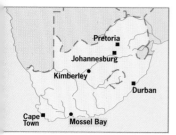

The Garden Route is one of the country's most scenic drives. Skirting the Indian Ocean, and occasionally dipping inland through lush nature reserves, across high passes and past lakes, lagoons, bays and mountains, this is a coast of holiday resorts. Accommodation in hotels, self-catering cottages, caravan parks and camp sites, is plentiful, and there are opportunities for a huge variety of sport from golfing to windsurfing. *Allow at least a weekend.*

Start at Mossel Bay.

1 MOSSEL BAY

The staple diet of the Khoikhoi inhabitants of this area, now a boomtown following the discovery of offshore oil, was mussels – hence its name. Nearly 500 years ago, the custom was begun whereby passing ships deposited letters and documents in the trunk of a milkwood tree (which still stands) for collection by other seafarers. This early history is documented in the town's museums.

Continue on the N2 for about 38km, then branch left (N12) to George – 10km. The Wilderness National Park straddles the N2 east of George.

2 GEORGE AND THE WILDERNESS NATIONAL PARK

At the foot of the Outeniqua Mountains, George, founded in 1811, was named after George III. One of the principal towns of the Garden Route, it grew up as an administrative and timber centre. It has some early buildings and a museum

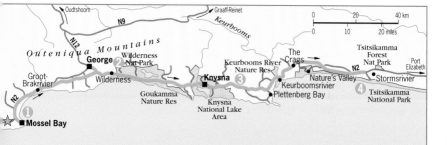

Knysna, on its beautiful 17km lagoon, is a holiday resort in a glorious setting

detailing the area's indigenous timber resources. The Wilderness National Park protects a wetlands ecosystem from encroaching development by weekenders, with whom the Wilderness resort is very popular. This is an area favoured by birdwatchers, ramblers, hikers and anglers. A magnificent rail route exists between George and neighbouring Knysna (see page 137). *Continue on the N2 to Knysna, 61km.*

3 KNYSNA AND PLETTENBERG BAY

Situated in an area of great scenic beauty, Knysna is a holiday resort sprawled along the northern banks of a large lagoon. Open to the sea between two large sandstone cliffs called The Heads, the lagoon is a major source of oysters. With a large variety of fish, the fishing is excellent. The Knysna Forest (36,400 hectares), South Africa's largest expanse of indigenous high forest containing giant yellowwood and stinkwood trees, is home to an elusive herd of Cape bush elephant. George Rex, reputedly George III's illegitimate son, is Knysna's most famous former resident – the museum is filled with his memorabilia. East of Knysna (30km), Plettenberg Bay is one of South Africa's most fashionable beach resorts.

Continue east on the N2 to the Tsitsikamma National Park.

4 TSITSIKAMMA NATIONAL PARK

In 1964, an 80km stretch of the southern Cape coastline, plus an area stretching out into the sea for 5.5km, were set apart as a reserve for terrestrial and marine flora and fauna. Its name is Khoikhoi for 'place of the many waters'. Once this region was covered entirely by indigenous forest which still survives in areas (see the 800-year-old yellowwood tree in the Tsitsikamma Forest).

Bartholomieu Dias Museum Complex, Market Street, Mossel Bay. Tel: 0444–911067. Open: weekdays 9am–5pm, Saturday 10am–1pm.
George Museum, Courtenay Street, George. Tel: 0441–735343. Open: weekdays 9am–4.30pm, Saturday 9am–12.30pm.
Wilderness National Park, 15km east of George. Tel: 0441–877 1197.
Knysna Museum, Queen Street. Tel: 0445–22133. Open: Monday to Saturday 8.30am–5pm.
Tsitsikamma National Park: National Parks Board. Tel: 012–343 1991. See Parks and Reserves, page 185.

THE SAN

Formerly known as Bushmen, the San are short in stature, relatively light in colour and have high cheekbones and tightly curled hair. Nomadic hunters and gatherers, they are closely related to the Khoikhoi (Hottentots) who were semi-nomadic hunters and pastoralists. The impact of white settlement – particularly outbreaks of smallpox in the 18th century – had a devastating effect on their population and today there are few pure San. Many interbred with other racial groups and their descendants are now considered a part of the 'Coloured' population.

Thousands of years ago, the San were spread across virtually all of Southern Africa. Following the advance of other black, then white races, they were driven into the Kalahari Desert of the Northern Cape and Botswana, and parts of northern Namibia, where 4,000 to 5,000 still live as did their Late Stone Age ancestors,

The San way of life goes back millennia, as their ancient rock art shows

in small bands, tracking and hunting with bows and poisoned arrows, collecting moisture-bearing plants and storing water in ostrich egg shells. Africa's only surviving hunter-gatherer lifestyle, San culture in its untainted form can be found only in tiny pockets scattered around Botswana.

The San have a rich tradition of story-telling, music and dancing; their language is characterised by click consonants, thought to derive from South Nguni interaction with the San. The Xhosa employed them as rainmakers, and many elements of Xhosa religious and healing systems have been borrowed from the San.

Evidence of the early San is plentiful in South Africa. Although painting is now, sadly, an art they have lost, San cave rock paintings and engravings depicting hunting and animal migration scenes are well known, particularly in the foothills of the Drakensberg and in the mountains of the Western Cape. Dating these with accuracy was difficult, until the discovery in the Wonderwerk Caves near Kuruman of engraved stone fragments identified as 10,000 years old. The earliest datable painting is about 28,000 years old.

Free State, Northern Cape and the Northwest

*T*hese three regions represent the extremes of South Africa's geography and landscape. Together they account for nearly half the country's land mass. This is an area associated with the early San and Khoikhoi, and with diamonds and gold. Sparsely populated, it is relatively undervisited by all but the hardiest of travellers and those in search of vast horizons, space and utter silence.

The arid, desolate landscape of the Northern Cape offers the greatest drama. A region where the air is fresh and unpolluted, it is best visited in the spring when the Namaqualand area centred on Springbok is enlivened by displays of millions of colourful wild flowers. The Northern Cape was once populated by nomadic San and Khoikhoi herders; their art adorns the walls of remote caves.

Landlocked Free State was an independent republic throughout much of the 19th century. Its capital is Bloemfontein, founded on the site of a prolific natural spring which was once a focus of survival for game, early indigenous people and the pioneers. In

The elegant kudu, one of the largest of the southern African antelopes

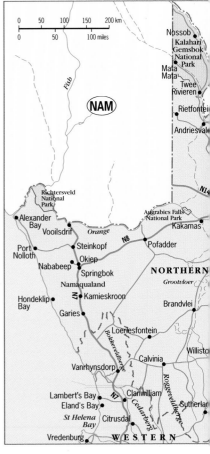

its northern reaches, Free State is richly fertile while the south is a region of grassy plains, farmlands, isolated mountains, rocky hillocks and small, tranquil towns. Far away on the frontiers with KwaZulu/Natal and Lesotho, the remote Highlands are alive in spring with wild flowers, blossom and herbs.

The Northwest is prairie land. There are rolling fields of sunflowers and maize, and bushveld dotted with thorn trees stretches as far as the eye can see. Here are some of South Africa's biggest cattle and game ranches. The Pilanesberg and the nearby resort of Sun City attract gamblers, walkers and anybody seeking respite from the drama of urban Johannesburg just to the east.

FREE STATE, NORTHERN CAPE & THE NORTHWEST

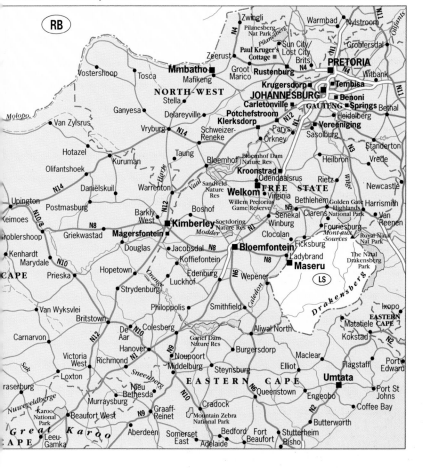

AUGRABIES FALLS NATIONAL PARK

The mighty Orange River dominates life in the arid Northern Cape, where water is precious. After a slow crawl across Africa to the Atlantic, it enters the 82,000-hectare Augrabies Falls National Park where it plunges into an 18km ravine and over a series of thundering falls (the fifth largest in the world) which take their name from the Khoikhoi '*aukoerebis*' ('place of great noise'). A viewing suspension bridge straddles the main cataract. There is game here too, and plantlife includes the remarkable 'kokerboom' (quiver tree). The three-day Klipspringer Trail is popular.
120km west of Upington. National Parks Board. Tel: 012–44 1191.

BLOEMFONTEIN

Bloemfontein, South Africa's judicial headquarters, occupies the site of the farm Bloem Fonteyn ('fountain of the flowers'). The President Brand Street Conservation Area preserves a section of early Bloemfontein, and museums include Freshford House (built 1897), a monument to colonial Victoriana, and the National Museum with collections of fossils and archaeological material. The Queen's Fort (1848), a British stronghold in the Basotho War, houses the Military Museum. The National Women's Memorial and War Museum is a grim reminder of the 1899–1902 Anglo-Boer War concentration camps in which an estimated 26,000 Afrikaner women and children died, mostly from disease and hunger. Emily Hobhouse did much to alleviate their suffering, and brought their plight to the attention of the British Government. An estimated 14,000 blacks died in separate camps.
398km southwest of Johannesburg.
Bloemfontein Publicity Association, PO Box 639, Bloemfontein 9300. Tel: 051–405 8489. Freshford House, 31 Kellner Street. Tel: 051–479609, ext 240. Open: weekdays 10am–1pm, weekends 2–5pm. Admission charge. National Museum, corner of Charles and Aliwal streets. Tel: 051–479609. Open: Monday to Saturday 8am–5pm, Sunday 1–6pm. Admission charge. Queen's Fort, Church Street. Tel: 051–475478. Open: weekdays 8am–4pm. Admission charge. National Women's Memorial and War Museum, Monument Road. Tel: 051–473447. Open: weekdays 9am–4.30pm, Saturday 9am–5pm, Sunday 2–5pm. Admission charge.

EASTERN HIGHLANDS

The Golden Gate Highlands National Park (see page 72) is the main attraction here, while in neighbouring Qwa Qwa National Park the Basotho Cultural Village provides an insight into Sotho culture, albeit theme-park style. South of Harrismith, a prosperous

A pleasant corner of Bloemfontein, South Africa's judicial capital

Wide open spaces in the Harrismith-Bethlehem area – good riding country

agricultural centre at the heart of magnificent riding country, is the 18,000-hectare Sterkfontein Dam Nature Reserve with game-viewing, birdwatching, watersports and hiking. Clarens is a quaint village (founded 1912) named after the Swiss town where President Kruger died, and Bethlehem, near Loch Athlone, is a centre for fishing, boating and swimming. Fouriesburg (founded 1892), a stronghold of the Boer forces in the Anglo-Boer War, is in an eccentric landscape dotted with sandstone flat-topped hillocks.

Qwa Qwa National Park, east of Royal Natal National Park (Highlands Development, Eco-Tourism Division). Tel: 058–713 4444. Sterkfontein Dam Nature Reserve. Tel: 05861–23520.

GARIEF DAM

On the banks of the huge dam of the Orange and Caledon rivers are three important nature reserves with accommodation and activities ranging from birdwatching and game-viewing to sailing and swimming. All three are different: the Garief Dam Nature Reserve is an arid Karoo environment of *koppies* and rocky outcrops; in Oviston Nature Reserve animals, particularly Burchell's zebra and the black wildebeest, are bred to stock other conservation areas; and Tussen-die-Riviere, situated at the confluence of the Orange and the Caledon rivers, is a vast expanse of veld dotted with rocky outcrops and massive boulders. Here there are wide, magnificent night skies much appreciated by the San. At Aasvoelkop, a prominent *koppie* near the eastern edge of the reserve, some of their rock paintings have been preserved.

About 160km south of Bloemfontein. Tel: 052171–26. Tussen-die-Riviere. Tel: 051762–2803.

Sandstone cliffs overlook a rest camp in Golden Gate Highlands National Park

GOLDEN GATE HIGHLANDS NATIONAL PARK

This 4,792-hectare reserve harbours a landscape of brilliant yellow, orange and red 'Clarens' sandstone cliffs, high outcrops and caves, pummelled into bizarre shapes by water. Here the early San hunters sheltered when not roaming the central plains in search of game, until driven out by early Iron Age Bantu groups (later called the Sotho), who settled on the secure heights of the high outcrop 'fortresses'. Today the reserve shelters, among other animals, eland, black wildebeest and springbok, and there are black eagles and jackal buzzards. Opportunities exist for hiking, trout fishing, riding, camping, caravanning, and there are two rest camps with chalets or huts.

Approximately 360km south of Johannesburg, *300km northeast of Bloemfontein. National Parks Board, PO Box 787, Pretoria 0001. Tel: 012–343 1991. Admission charge.*

KALAHARI GEMSBOK NATIONAL PARK

Lying northwest of Upington, where the rust-red Kalahari Desert is so porous that rain or dew sinks and vanishes immediately, this is South Africa's remotest game park. It extends into Botswana, covering over three million hectares and is one of the largest unspoilt ecosystems in the world. It was founded in the 1930s to curb the activities of poachers and to provide a haven for the spectacular Cape oryx, or gemsbok. Only three roads penetrate the region – two of them running along riverbeds where

The gemsbok, or oryx

much of the wildlife is concentrated. Apart from elephant, giraffe and zebra, practically every other species of game can be found here – including dark-maned Kalahari lion, cheetah and leopard – and over 215 species of birds from ostrich to the kori bustard have been recorded. Rest camps at Twee Rivieren, Mata Mata and Nossob have accommodation ranging from chalets to campsites, and there are places to eat and picnic.
358km northwest of Upington. The Mata Mata gate from Namibia is closed. National Parks Board. Tel: 012–419 5365. Admission charge.

KIMBERLEY

In July 1871 the first Kimberley diamond was discovered at Colesberg Kopje, around which Kimberley, initially a tent town called New Rush, was to develop (see pages 76–7). The site became Kimberley Mine, later the Big Hole, the largest man-made excavation anywhere, which yielded three tons of diamonds. Today it is part of the open-air Kimberley Mine Museum which incorporates entire streets of turn-of-the-century buildings. In 1869 diamonds were discovered on Bultfontein farm; today the Bultfontein Mine is part of De Beers Consolidated Mines Ltd and surface tours of the treatment and recovery plant take place daily. Diamonds aside, Kimberley has three other important venues: the McGregor Museum, detailing the history and environment of the Northern Cape; the Duggan-Cronin Gallery, which details tribal life in South Africa; and the William Humphreys Art Gallery with a collection of South African art.

Magersfontein is the site of one of the worst British defeats in the Anglo-Boer War (1899). The battlesite has a small museum.

Kimberley is about 670km southwest of Johannesburg. Kimberley Tourist Information, City Hall, Market Square. Tel: 0531–80 6264. Bultfontein Mine, Molyneux Road. Tel: 0531–29651, mornings only. Open: tours, weekdays 9am and 11am. Admission charge. Advance booking essential. No children under 8. Kimberley Mine Museum and Big Hole, Tucker Street. Tel: 0531–31557. Open: daily 8am–6pm. Admission charge. McGregor Museum, Atlas Street. Tel: 0531–32645. Open: weekdays 9am–5pm, Saturday 9am–1pm, 2–5pm, Sunday 2–5pm. Admission charge. Duggan-Cronin Gallery, Egerton Road. Tel: 0531–32645. Open: weekdays 9am–5pm, Saturday 9am–1pm, 2–5pm, Sunday 2–5pm. Admission charge. Magersfontein Battlefield, 32km on the Modder River road. Tel: 0531–22029. Admission charge.

Street in the Kimberley Mine Museum

tribe, once noted for metal-working skills. Okiep (from '*U-gieb*', 'brackish') has a copper mine once the world's richest; the years of peak demand led to the industrialisation, such as it is, of Namaqualand. South of Springbok, Kamieskroon and the region between it and Hondeklip Bay yield rich panoramas of spring flowers.

Springbok is 559km north of Cape Town. Namaqualand Regional Tourism Office, PO Box 5, Springbok. Tel: 0251–22011. Richtersveld National Park, access via Springbok, Steinkopf, Port Nolloth and Alexander Bay, from which it is 93km. Tel: 0256–506.

PILANESBERG NATIONAL PARK

Situated in what was once the Bophuthatswana Homeland, is Pilanesberg National Park. Easily accessible from Pretoria and Johannesburg, the park makes a good weekend destination. South Africa's fifth largest, it sprawls over 500sq km, an impressive controlled 'wilderness' where the Pilanesberg mountains crowd around Lake Mankwe. It was formed in the 1970s, replacing farmland and creating welcome sanctuary for elephant, giraffe, white and black rhino, hippo, buffalo, leopard and cheetah. Accommodation is plentiful, ranging from timeshare resorts to self-catering chalets and camp sites, and there are plenty of picnic spots, hides and so on.

Sun City and Lost City

The park is easily accessible from both Sun City and The Lost City, two hotel-casino resorts. Sun City is older and blander than the huge, opulent Lost

NAMAQUALAND

A vast area of the Northern Cape's huge semi-desert is a Cinderella environment. Most of the year it is harsh and dry, but after the winter rainfall (mid-August to mid-September is best) it is transformed by millions of brightly coloured daisies, mesembryanthemums, aloes and lilies. Springbok, the region's 'capital', once a waterhole for springbok, is ideally situated for wild flower excursions and visits to the Richtersveld National Park. In the province's northwestern corner where population is sparse, the park is a botanist's paradise, with 50 per cent of its plants rarities and almost certainly other species as yet undiscovered.

It is the park's distinctive flora that rank it as one of the nation's best sights. The mountain desert scenery here is arid, rocky and pitted with ravines, home to the semi-nomadic Nama, a Khoikhoi

City, which tries to re-create Rider Haggard's turn-of-the-century novel *King Solomon's Mines*. 'Kitsch' is not a word that adequately describes the scene, but it is fun, if you don't mind the appalling poverty at the gates. Sun City's attractions include the Valley of the Waves, a huge landlocked watersports area with electronically induced waves, and the Arizona desert-style golf course.

Pilanesberg National Park is about 100km west of Pretoria. Tel: 01465–5534. Manyane Gate is the main entrance and information centre. Admission charge.

SANDVELD NATURE RESERVE

Surrounding the Bloemhof Dam, this is one of the best of Free State's reserves. Raw Africa is here, where the majestic thorn trees of the Kalahari thornveld provide cover for small mammals like aardwolf, antbears, porcupines and springhare. Gemsbok, blue wildebeest, white rhino, giraffe and kudu also thrive here, and the dam attracts ibis, flamingo and other waterbirds. White-backed vultures breed in large nests on top of the thorn trees. There are places to camp, holiday chalets and during the day activities range from game-watching to swimming and angling.

87km northwest of Bloemfontein. Tel: 01802–31701. Admission charge.

WILLEM PRETORIUS GAME RESERVE

Two rivers divide this 12,000-hectare reserve into northern and southern sections, and their confluence forms the Allemanskraal Dam. The hilly northern end with its dense vegetation supports baboons, bushbuck, kudu and duiker, while the southern end is truly 'teeming with wildlife'. Both are worth visiting: accommodation is in chalets and in a caravan park, and there is a restaurant.

150km northeast of Bloemfontein. Tel: 05777–4003. Admission charge.

The giraffe's neck enables it to browse the tops of its favourite acacia trees

DIAMONDS

The discovery of diamonds marked a turning-point in southern Africa's development from a rural, forgotten corner, dominated by the British Empire, to a depository of riches that in time would touch the lives of nearly everyone in the region. Diamonds are still a source of South Africa's wealth.

The first diamond discovered was the *Eureka* (1867), near Hopetown in the Northern Cape; further finds occurred in 1869 on the farms Bultfontein and Dorstfontein, owned by the De Beers family. In 1871 fabulously rich finds were made at Colesberg Kopje, which eventually led to the development of Kimberley (see page 73). Life was probably hell for the fortune-seekers who had flocked to the site, though some of them did indeed make fortunes – and not just as prospectors. Entrepreneurs started coaching companies, or provided such necessities as bars.

The biggest headache of all was establishing ownership of this diamond-rich territory. Called Griqualand West, it was claimed by the Griqua, who had lived there for 70 years, by the respective governments of the Free State and the South African Republic, and by the Cape Colony. In the end the British simply annexed it to the Cape (1880).

Kimberley was the cradle of the hugely profitable diamond industry that grew up in southern Africa

No-one could ever have dreamt of the riches that the Big Hole would yield. As digging continued, and the hole got deeper, squabbles broke out as miners struggled to get to their claims at ever more perilous depths. This led to the amalgamation of smaller workings, heralding the era of the big mining companies. About 20 years after the first diamond had been discovered, the De Beers mine, controlled by Cecil John Rhodes, owned virtually the entire diamond industry. In recent years, under Ernest and Harry Oppenheimer, it has become one of the world's largest and most profitable mining companies.

The Diamond Route

Kimberley was the focus of South Africa's early diamond boom, though not the only scene of lucrative finds. A range of other towns and locations associated with mining – and not exclusively of diamonds – are worth a visit. This tour takes in some of them. *Allow 2 to 3 days.*

Start at Kimberley.

1 KIMBERLEY
See page 73.
Barkly West lies 32km northwest of Kimberley on the R31.

2 BARKLY WEST
A cairn on Canteen Koppie marks the site of the first alluvial diamond diggings in South Africa (1869). The diggers, hoping to protect their claims, formed the Klip Drift Republic, with Stafford Parker as president. The Republic's short life ended when the British exerted their authority in December 1870. The diggings, like others along the Vaal River, unearthed large numbers of fossils and Stone Age implements (now in the Mining Commissioner's Museum). The site is now a national

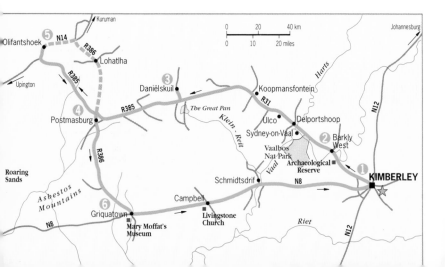

Cliffs along the Olifants river valley

monument. In the town, St Mary's Church (built 1871) is filled with memories of the diggers. About 27km to the west, at Sydney-on-Vaal near the Vaalbos National Park, is Sydney Village, a diamond boom tent town (1896). Here, too, you can indulge in some diamond panning.
Continue on the R31 for 123km to Daniëlskuil.

3 DANIËLSKUIL

A sinkhole used as a prison gave this town its name, which translates as 'Daniel's Den'. Snakes rather than lions provided the punishment, and anyone who survived the night was considered to have proved his innocence. Asbestos, diamonds and marble are the source of Daniëlskuil's prosperity. Diamonds – 26 in the first two hours of prospecting – were discovered here in 1960.
Take the R31 and proceed south for 10km, then turn west and proceed on the R385 to Postmasburg, 49km.

4 POSTMASBURG

Postmasburg has its own 'big hole' – the old Postmas Diamond Mine which was worked successfully until 1935. It began life as a meerkat burrow, the first diamond being found in it in 1918. The West End Diamond Mine can be visited, as can the ancient mine workings on the slope of the Gatkoppies which, according to archaeological evidence, were worked by the Khoikhoi around AD700. Valuable deposits of manganese and iron ore have also been extracted here. Mine and workings can be visited by appointment only.
Proceed north on the R385 for 54km to Olifantshoek.

5 OLIFANTSHOEK

Named after the elephant whose tusks were used as payment for the ground on which it stands, Olifantshoek is located on the route to the Roaring Sands. These 100m-high dunes produce an uncanny moaning if disturbed during dry, hot weather. Below the surface of the white sands is found pure, sweet water.
Return to Postmasburg on the R385 (or via the 27km stretch of the N14, then for 50km on the R386), then continue to Griquatown on the R386 (96km).

6 GRIQUATOWN

This settlement, dwarfed by the Asbestos Mountains, is best known as a mission station, which grew up around a Griqua settlement, and birthplace of Mary Moffat, wife of David Livingstone. Her birthplace, the old mission house, is now the Mary Moffat's Museum. Griquatown is also famous for gemstones, including tiger's-eye, a stone fairly common in these parts. See them at Earth Treasures.
Return to Kimberley on the N8 (158km).

Mary Moffat's Museum, Voortrekker Street, Griquatown. Open: weekdays 8am–5pm. Admission charge.
Earth Treasures, Moffat Street, Griquatown. Tel: 05962, ask for 121. Open: weekdays 7.30am–5pm. Admission charge.

Northern Province, Mpuma-langa, KwaZulu/Natal

*T*he Africa of ancient traditions and magic, the 19th-century South Africa of the great Zulu Kingdom and the Anglo-Boer Wars, and the tourist delights of modern South Africa come together in the regions covered here.

Of all the regions of South Africa, it is in the far north that old Africa is most alive. In an area of wide open plains and majestic mountains, primeval indigenous forests and latter-day plantations, a tradition of rain-making survives, the preserve of an hereditary princess (see page 105). Near by is an ancient lake, the haunt of a spirit and out of bounds to all but the tribe who, in their ancestral lands, care for a forest of primeval cycads, primitive plants that were once the food of dinosaurs.

Mpumalanga (Eastern Transvaal) is different. From the Witwatersrand and Pretoria, the high plateau grasslands of the Transvaal Midlands stretch eastward for hundreds of kilometres. In the northeast, the plateau rises towards mountain peaks, then terminates in an immense escarpment which plunges

The high-rise skyline of fast-growing Durban as seen from North Beach

abruptly down to the Lowveld, a land of pioneers and adventurers, and scene of the earliest gold rush. Northeast of Graskop, God's Window provides a view on thickly forested mountains, the lush and fertile Lowveld, waterfalls and lakes.

KwaZulu/Natal stretches from the southern borders of Swaziland and Mozambique to the northern border of the Eastern Cape in the south. It is bounded by the Indian Ocean in the east and on the west by Lesotho, the Free State and the Transvaal. The magnificent Drakensberg Mountains dramatically straddle the borders. This region has great diversity of landscape. From the lush hills and pastures of the Natal Midlands to untamed wildernesses in the north which focus on a range of precious reserves, to the broad sandy beaches fringed with subtropical forest, it is a country of vast natural riches. There are parks and reserves scattered throughout, all accessible from Durban.

NORTH PROV, MPUMALANGA, KWAZULU/NATAL

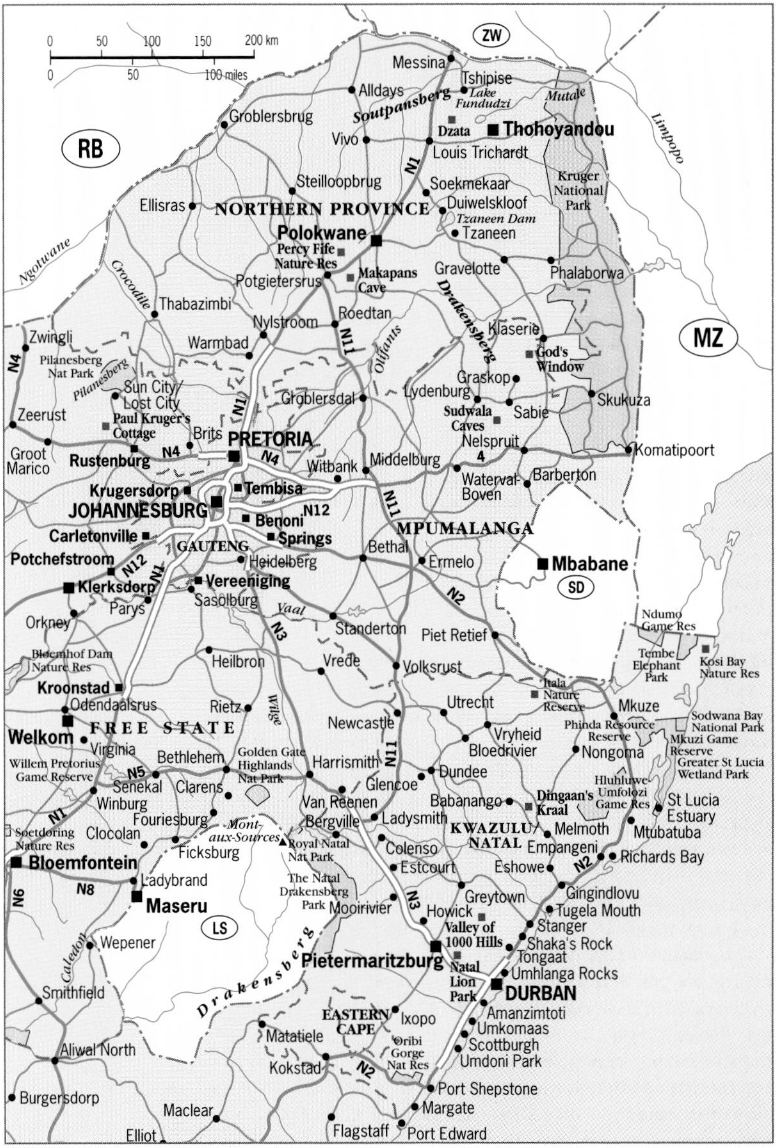

Map legend and labels:

0 50 100 150 200 km
0 50 100 miles

ZW

Messina
Tshipise
Lake Fundudzi
Mutale
Alldays
Soutpansberg
Groblersbrug
Vivo
Dzata
Thohoyandou
Louis Trichardt
Limpopo
RB
Steilloopbrug
Soekmekaar
Duiwelskloof
Kruger National Park
Ellisras
NORTHERN PROVINCE
Tzaneen Dam
Tzaneen
Polokwane
Percy Fife Nature Res
Makapans Cave
Gravelotte
Phalaborwa
Potgietersrus
Thabazimbi
Nylstroom
Roedtan
Klaserie
Drakensberg
MZ
Zwingli
Pilanesberg Nat Park
Warmbad
God's Window
Ngotwane
Crocodile
Pilanesberg
Sun City
Lost City
Groblersdal
Lydenburg
Graskop
Skukuza
Zeerust
Paul Kruger's Cottage
Brits
Oliphants
Sudwala Caves
Sabie
Groot Marico
Rustenburg
PRETORIA
N4
Witbank
Middelburg
Nelspruit
Komatipoort
N4
Waterval Boven
Barberton
Krugersdorp
Tembisa
N12
JOHANNESBURG
Benoni
Springs
GAUTENG
Bethal
Ermelo
MPUMALANGA
Mbabane
Carletonville
Heidelberg
SD
Potchefstroom
Vereeniging
Ndumo Game Res
Klerksdorp
Sasolburg
Vaal
Tembe Elephant Park
Kosi Bay Nature Res
Orkney
Parys
Standerton
Piet Retief
Bloemhof Dam Nature Res
Heilbron
Vrede
Volksrust
Kroonstad
Wilge
Utrecht
Mkuze
Sodwana Bay National Park
Odendaalsrus
Rietz
Newcastle
Vryheid
Phinda Resource Reserve
Welkom
FREE STATE
Bloedrivier
Nongoma
Mkuzi Game Reserve
Virginia
Bethlehem
Golden Gate Highlands Nat Park
Harrismith
Glencoe
Dundee
Babanango
Hluhluwe
Umfolozi Game Res
Greater St Lucia Wetland Park
Senekal
Clarens
Van Reenen
Ladysmith
Dingaan's Kraal
Melmoth
St Lucia Estuary
Winburg
Fouriesburg
Bergville
KWAZULU/
Mtubatuba
Soetdoring Nature Res
Clocolan
Mont-aux-Sources
Royal Natal Nat Park
Colenso
NATAL
Empangeni
Bloemfontein
Ficksburg
The Natal Drakensberg Park
Estcourt
Eshowe
Richards Bay
Maseru
Ladybrand
Mooirivier
Gingindlovu
LS
Greytown
Howick
Tugela Mouth
Wepener
Pietermaritzburg
Valley of 1000 Hills
Stanger
Smithfield
Natal Lion Park
Shaka's Rock
Tongaat
Umhlanga Rocks
DURBAN
Aliwal North
EASTERN CAPE
Ixopo
Amanzimtoti
Matatiele
Oribi Gorge Nat Res
Umkomaas
Scottburgh
Burgersdorp
Kokstad
Umdoni Park
Maclear
Port Shepstone
Margate
Elliot
Flagstaff
Port Edward

Drakensberg
Caledon

N1 N2 N3 N4 N5 N6 N8 N11 N12

Durban

*B*anana City to some, eThegwini to the Zulus, and Durban to everyone else, this is the world's fastest growing metropolis after Mexico City, and Africa's largest port.

Spread along the ocean's edge, Durban used to have an image as a bastion of respectability and outpost of the British Empire. Today, apartheid is gone and the multiple diversity of the city's culture is confidently showing its face. Here Asia and Europe meet Africa. It is a frenetic, colourful and cosmopolitan city bursting at the seams.

On the edge of traditional Zulu territory, Durban was once called Port Natal. From it, Britain colonised Natal, and to it were brought indentured labourers from India whose descendants are largely responsible for endowing the city with a huge portion of its distinctive character. Durban might be the focal point of one of South Africa's most popular coastal resorts, but behind its 'Golden Mile' are mosques, temples and exotic oriental-style bazaars. These abut ponderous Victorian architecture and add to the rich variety of an urban environment already enlivened by the colourful Zulu regalia of the rickshaw men and the open-air markets piled with baskets and beadwork, tin pots and ethnic sculpture.

There is also a sophisticated yacht club, and a cult devoted to surfing – a sport practised to world renown right on the edge of the city. In spite of all this – and its theatres, thriving business centre and ebullient nightlife – Durban is not the capital of the province. That title belongs to Pietermaritzburg.

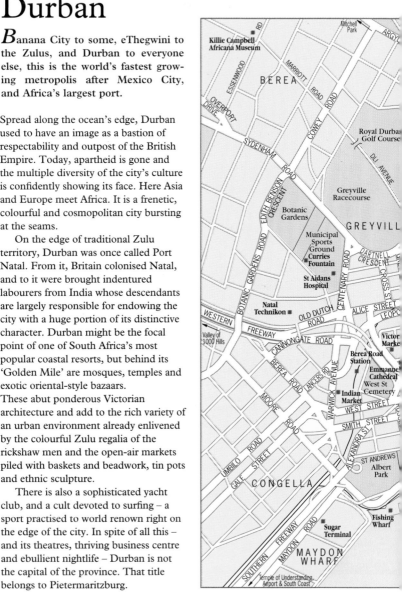

DURBAN

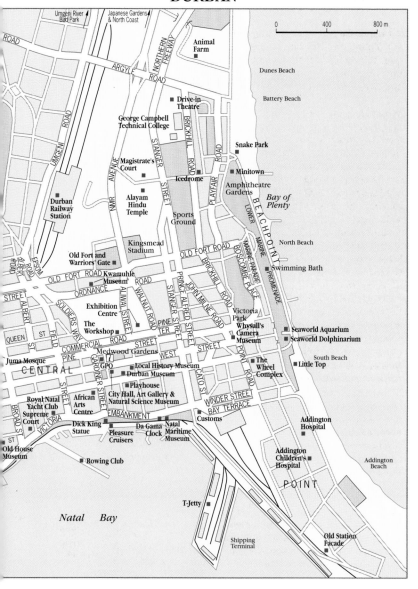

Umgeni River / Bird Park
Japanese Gardens / & North Coast

ROAD

ARGYLE ROAD

NORTHERN FREEWAY

Animal Farm

Dunes Beach

Battery Beach

Drive-in Theatre

BRICKHILL ROAD

George Campbell Technical College

Snake Park

STANGER STREET

Magistrate's Court

Minitown

Icedrome

PLAYFAIR

Amphitheatre Gardens

Bay of Plenty

NMR AVENUE

UMGENI ROAD

Alayam Hindu Temple

LOWER MARINE

BEACH POINT

Durban Railway Station

Sports Ground

North Beach

Kingsmead Stadium

OLD FORT ROAD

MARINE PARADE

Old Fort and Warriors' Gate

Kwamuhle Museum

BRICKHILL ROAD

Swimming Bath

BOSCOMBE PLACE

EPSOM ROAD

ALBERT ROAD

OLD FORT ROAD

ORDNANCE ROAD

WALNUT ROAD

JOHN MILNE ROAD

PROMENADE

STREET

SOLDIERS' WAY

Exhibition Centre

ALIWAL STREET

PINE TER

STANGER STREET

PRINCE ALFRED STREET

Victoria Park

ALBERT STREET

The Workshop

Whysall's Camera Museum

Seaworld Aquarium

QUEEN ST

FIELD

COMMERCIAL ROAD

STREE

WEST STREET

POINT ROAD

Seaworld Dolphinarium

Juma Mosque

PINE

Medwood Gardens

South Beach

CENTRAL

GARDINER STREET

GPO

Local History Museum

Durban Museum

CATO'S RD

The Wheel Complex

Little Top

Playhouse

Royal Natal Yacht Club

BROAD ST

VICTORIA

African Arts Centre

City Hall, Art Gallery & Natural Science Museum

WINDER STREET

Supreme Court

EMBANKMENT

BAY TERRACE

Addington Hospital

ST

Dick King Statue

Da Gama Clock

Natal Maritime Museum

Customs

Old House Museum

Pleasure Cruisers

Addington Children's Hospital

Addington Beach

Rowing Club

POINT

Natal Bay

T-Jetty

Shipping Terminal

Old Station Façade

0   400   800 m

Durban City Hall, once the epitome of the Empire, now a repository for native art

Sydenham Road, Berea. Open: daily 9.30am–12.30pm, 2.30–5pm. Admission charge.

DURBAN CITY HALL, ART GALLERY AND MUSEUM

Durban's City Hall was built in 1910 as a replica of Northern Ireland's Belfast City Hall. It commands a dominant position facing Francis Farewell Square, where the two entrepreneurs Henry Flynn and Francis Farewell established a company in 1824, trading ivory with the Zulus. The City Hall, a bombastic affair trumpeting the might of Empire, is now a centre of great cultural wealth. It houses the Durban Art Gallery with displays of contemporary South African art and applied art and craft; its collection of geometrically patterned so-called *hlabisa* baskets is unsurpassed. Although it also contains, among other things, Victorian paintings and French and Chinese ceramics, it is the first gallery in South Africa to collect black art seriously. The Natural Science Museum has exhibits illustrating the natural history of KwaZulu/Natal, and includes the most complete known skeleton of the extinct dodo, as well as a horrifying display of cockroaches – in South Africa these insects are often of monstrous proportions.
City Hall, Smith Street. Tel: 031–300 6911. Durban Art Gallery and Natural Science Museum – both open: Monday to Saturday 8.30am–5pm, Sunday 11am–5pm. Admission charge.

GOLDEN MILE

Along 6km between Addington Beach and Blue Lagoon are Durban's best

AFRICAN ART CENTRE

This non-profit gallery concentrates on the work of local black artists who, in the townships and squatter camps, make basketware, woven cloth, prints, pottery and bead sculptures. Some of the items are of exceptional quality and, even if you don't want to buy, it is worthwhile browsing. This centre has information about other similar locations in the area.
8 Guildhall Arcade, 35 Gardiner Street. Tel: 031–304 7915. Open: Monday to Thursday 8.30am–5pm, Friday 8.30am–4pm, Saturday 8.30am–12.30pm.

BOTANIC GARDENS AND ORCHID HOUSE

Well known for its orchid house – its vast collection exceeds 3,000 plants – and collection of cycads, the Botanic Garden incorporates a lovely wooded garden and a magnificent jade vine.

beaches. The beachfront promenade is lively and – in the summer – busy. Nets protect the area from sharks, and life-savers protect swimmers from themselves. The surfing is excellent, and there are plenty of opportunities for enthusiasts to sail, fish, snorkel and scuba-dive. Hitch a ride on a rickshaw (see page 87), or visit Fitzsimon's Snake Park with its collection of snakes, crocodiles and iguanas, or the Amphitheatre Sunday fleamarket. There are hotels, nightclubs and restaurants and a multitude of street vendors hawking wares from beaded jewellery to painted ostrich eggs.

Fitzsimon's Snake Park, Snell Parade, North Beach. Tel: 031–37 6456. Open: daily 9am–4.30pm. Admission charge.

INDIAN DURBAN

Durban has a thriving Indian culture, and a rich Hindu and Muslim architectural heritage. The Grey Street trading area is a lively commercial quarter (see page 145) which, with its scents, sounds and brilliant colours, evokes the orient. Here, too, is the great Juma Mosque. The Group Areas Act or land expropriation oversaw the demolition of at least six Hindu temples. Of those that survive, two have been declared National Monuments: the Ganesha Temple at Mount Edgecombe and the Alayam Hindu Temple, the oldest (1875, rebuilt 1947) and biggest Hindu temple in South Africa. The latter contains some of the best examples of temple sculpture in the country.

Juma Mosque, 155 Queen Street. Tel: 031–306 1724. Ganesha Temple, Mount Edgecombe. Tel: 031–593 409. Shree Ambalvanar Alayam Second River Temple, Bellair Road. Tel: 031–593 409.

The African Art Centre functions as both a gallery and a shop

KILLIE CAMPBELL AFRICANA MUSEUM

Muckleneuk, the former home of sugar baron Sir Marshall Campbell, contains one of the country's best private libraries of Africana, collected by his daughter, Dr Margaret Roach Campbell. After her death in 1965, the house and its lovely grounds were donated to the University of Natal. There is an excellent collection of African musical instruments, beadwork, pottery, weapons and so on.
Berea Ridge, corner of Marriot and Essenwood roads. Tel: 031–207 3432. Open: Tuesday and Thursday 8am–1pm. Guided tours by appointment. Admission charge.

KWAMUHLE MUSEUM

This is the country's only museum to have as its central theme 20th-century South African urban social history. It continually documents and evaluates the changes that occur in Durban through the eyes of the majority of the city's residents – Africans. The museum is housed in the 1930s former Bantu Administration Board office, and is named KwaMuhle ('place of the good one') after J S Marwick who, during the Anglo-Boer War, helped 7,000 African migrants to leave the Transvaal and return to Natal and Zululand.
132 Ordnance Road. Tel: 031–300 6313. Open: Monday to Saturday 8.30am–5pm, Sunday 11am–5pm. Admission charge.

LOCAL HISTORY MUSEUM

From ships to buildings, period costume to colonial life, this museum housed in the old Court House (1863) provides an interesting view on the life and times of Durban. Temporary exhibitions are its strong point: recent ones have ranged from Durban's whaling industry to Gandhi's time in Natal (see page 103), from protest posters of human rights organisations to signs used during apartheid. There's a museum shop.
Aliwal Street. Tel: 031–300 6241. Open: Monday to Saturday 8.30am–5pm, Sundays and public holidays, 11am–5pm. Free.

NATAL MARITIME MUSEUM

The selection of boats in this museum is a reminder that, for all its beaches and languid beachlife, Durban is still a working port. There are two early tugs as well as a minesweeper from World War II (SAS *Durban*).
Victoria Embankment. Tel: 031–306 1092. Open: Monday to Saturday 8.30am–4pm, Sunday 11am–4pm. Admission charge.

OLD HOUSE MUSEUM

This museum of the Natal settlers, a replica of a settler homestead, contains a collection of colonial domestic items.
31 St Andrews Street. Tel: 031–300 6250.

Public pool on Durban's waterfront, an alternative to sea bathing

Open: Monday to Saturday
8.30am–5pm, Sunday
11am–5pm. Admission charge.

SEAWORLD AQUARIUM AND DOLPHINARIUM

While nets protect bathers
from sharks, here, at one of
the world's leading marine
research centres, you can
watch them feed, and see the
antics of dolphins, seals,
turtles – and much more.
Sea end of West Street. Tel:
031–37 3536. Open: daily
9am–9pm. Admission charge.

THE RICKSHAW MEN

A unique feature of the
Durban beachfront scene
is the two-wheeler carts
pulled by exotically
dressed Zulu rickshaw
drivers; for a small charge
you can ride in one.
Hugely popular with
tourists, they nonetheless
periodically threaten to
vanish from the scene.
Under apartheid they went
into a decline but are now
gradually being rescued as the city council and local businesses realise their pulling
power, so to speak. The rickshaws were introduced from Japan in 1893, and by 1904
some 2,000 thronged the streets transporting people as well as goods. The last
commercial one retired in the 1970s, and only a few extravagantly attired Zulus
continue the tradition – with the help of Nike running shoes.

WARRIORS' GATE

This has an excellent collection of
battlefield relics from this much fought-
over area, with medals, badges and other
military items. Near by, the Old Fort was
a bastion of the British forces under

attack from the Boers in 1842.
Warriors' Gate, Old Fort Road. Tel:
031–307 3337. Open: Tuesday to Saturday
8.30am–5pm, Sunday 11am–5pm. Old
Fort. Tel: 031–307 1776. Open: Monday
to Friday 10am–5pm.

BARBERTON

Barberton was founded following the discovery of gold on the Pioneer Reef (1884), but when news of gold discoveries on the Witwatersrand reached here the exodus was immediate, leaving the town deserted. Many of its old buildings survive, including Transvaal's first stock exchange (the Kaap Gold Fields Stock Exchange) and the 1887 Globe Tavern, a hostelry of a type common in the late 19th-century goldfields. Even some of the mines are still in operation. The museum contains artefacts relating to the gold rush days. In Barberton Park is a statue of the dog Jock, subject of Sir Percy FitzPatrick's famous story, *Jock of the Bushveld*.

To the north, Nelspruit, on the Crocodile River, is the commercial centre of the Lowveld and the hub of this citrus fruit region.

Barberton is 43km south of Nelspruit. Barberton Publicity Association, Main Street. Tel: 01314–24208. Barberton Museum, Pilgrim Street. Open: weekdays 9am–1pm, 2.30–4.45pm, Saturday 9am–5pm, Sunday 8.30am–noon. Admission charge.

DOLPHIN COAST

Warm, clear water and a shallow continental shelf off the coast between Umhlanga Rocks and the Tugela River Mouth create ideal conditions for the bottlenose and other species of dolphin, hence the coast's popular name. This is one of South Africa's favourite resort areas. There are game and bird reserves, miles of golden beaches, coves and rock pools.

Umhlanga Rocks is a resort with good surfing, one of the region's most popular beaches and the headquarters of the Natal Sharks Board (see box). Beyond Umhlanga, Umdloti (with its excellent natural rock pool for diving enthusiasts), Ballito (good surfing), Tongaat, La Mercy, Shaka's Rock and Salt Rock all have very safe bathing. Tongaat is predominantly Indian, with the country's oldest Hindu temple – the Juggernath Puri Temple (1901) – and Crocodile Creek, a crocodile conservation and breeding ranch on the Tongaat river. Shaka's Rock is where Shaka's warriors

The resort of Umhlanga Rocks, popular for its golden beach and good surfing

Surfing is just one of the many watersports enjoyed by enthusiasts on Durban's coast

proved their manhood by leaping into the sea. Salt Rock was where Zulu women collected salt from the pools now popular as swimming holes.

At Blythedale the beach is flat and totally unspoilt – perfect for swimming or fishing. Stanger is where Shaka established KwaDukuza (1825), a royal kraal of some 2,000 beehive huts, and was murdered by his half-brother Dingane (1828). At the Tugela River Mouth, just beyond lovely Zinkwazi Beach and lagoon, the Harold Johnson Nature Reserve focuses on the interaction between man and nature, and has an interesting museum of Nguni culture. Its Thukela Trail highlights various historical events and sites.
Umhlanga to Tugela River mouth is 90km. Dolphin Coast Publicity Association, PO Box 534, Ballito 4429. Tel: 0332–61997. Natal Sharks Board's audio-visual displays: Tuesday and Thursday at 9am, Wednesday 9am, 11am and 2.30pm, and the first Sunday of every month 2.30pm. Tel: 031–5611001. Admission charge. Crocodile Creek – tel: 0322–23845. Open: daily 10am–4.30pm. Admission charge. Harold Johnson Nature Reserve, PO Box 148, Darnall 4480. Tel: 0324–615 74.

NATAL SHARKS BOARD
Since its foundation in 1964, the Natal Sharks Board has used anti-shark nets to protect coastal beaches – though not all beaches are protected and there have been a number of incidents of swimmers being attacked by sharks. The nets, where they are used, are checked daily, live animals freed and dead sharks brought back for research purposes. Nonetheless, the nets remain a controversial environmental issue as they inadvertently trap dolphins and turtles. A daily audio-visual presentation on sharks is followed by a dissection of the largest predator found dead in the nets – the emphasis being on the Zambezi tiger, the great white and the ragged-tooth sharks.

The mighty Amphitheatre in the Drakensberg, a stage fit for cosmic drama

DRAKENSBERG MOUNTAINS

'uKhahlamba' ('barrier'), Drakensberg ('Dragon Mountains') – thus the Zulu and Afrikaans languages appropriately describe the drama of these huge mountains (see also Golden Gate Highlands National Park, page 72). In the Northern Drakensberg, Mont-aux-Sources (3,282m), looming over the 8,000-hectare Royal Natal National Park, is the souce of the 322km-long Tugela River and of seven others, one of which eventually joins a tributary of the great Orange River. Among the park's attractions are the Amphitheatre, an 8km basalt crescent flanked by the Sentinel (3,165m) and the Eastern Buttress peaks (3,047m); San rock paintings (Sigubudu Shelter and Cannibal caves); and a variety of mammals including jackals and otters. You can undertake one-day walks, overnight hikes or five-day trails, climb challenging peaks, or take to horseback. There is a full range of accommodation in the park, and limited camping on Mont-aux-Sources.

The Central Drakensberg area possesses a series of soaring peaks – Cathkin Peak (3,149m), Cathedral Peak (3,004m, reputed to be the easiest to climb), Champagne Castle (3,371m, one of the highest) – and the magnificent Giant's Castle Game Reserve. The foothills are home to the Ngwane people (a branch of the Nguni), who are closely related to the original Zulu clan and resemble them closely in dress and customs. They settled here in the 19th century following the *Mfecane* (see box, page 9). A 60km-long contour path, leads to Cathkin Peak which, to the Zulus, is Mdedelele ('make room for him') – the name they give to a bully. It dominates a rugged mass of mountains and foothills in the highest part of the Drakensberg, and is approached through the Sterkspruit Valley in the lower reaches of which are resorts, hotels and caravan parks. This is good walking and riding country, and many of the resorts have stables.

The 34,600-hectare Giant's Castle Game Reserve has splendid San rock art, with over 500 paintings in the Main Caves. The walking here is excellent: round walks base to base, between huts, make trails of more than one day possible. There is riding, trout fishing and birdwatching (look out for the rare bearded vulture and black eagle), and over 60 species of mammals to spot. Kamberg Nature Reserve, southeast of Giant's Castle, has excellent trout fishing. The reserve's office sells permits. The 4km Mooi River Trail here is one of few in South Africa designed for the physically handicapped.

The Royal Natal National Park is about 30km west of Bergville (Natal Parks Board). Drakensberg Publicity Association, PO Box 325, Bergville 3350. Tel: 036–448 1557. Giant's Castle Game Reserve, 69km southwest of Estcourt (Natal Parks Board). Kamberg Nature Reserve, 42km west of Rosetta (Natal Parks Board).

ESTCOURT

At picturesque Estcourt (named after British MP Thomas Estcourt) is Fort Durnford, built on a *koppie* high above the Bushman River in 1847, to guard the ford and protect new settlers from marauding San who descended from their Drakensberg caves to steal cattle and, later, from the Zulus intent on defying colonial authority. It is now a museum in whose grounds is a reconstructed Zulu village. Estcourt is close to the Central Drakensberg, with good hiking and fishing. Colenso, north of Estcourt, is on the site of a Voortrekker *laager* attacked by Dingane's impis in 1838. Near by, the Armoured Train Memorial commemorates the occasion in 1899 when Winston Churchill, as a war correspondent, was captured following the derailment of the armoured train in which he was travelling.

Estcourt is 35km south of Colenso. It is 19.7km to the Armoured Train Memorial. Estcourt Tourist Information, PO Box 15, Estcourt 3310. Tel: 0363–23000. Fort Durnford Museum. Tel: 0363–23000 ext 253. Open: weekdays 9am–noon, 1–4pm. Admission charge.

Landscape in the Central Drakensberg beneath 3,004m-high Cathedral Peak

GREATER ST LUCIA WETLAND PARK

The Greater St Lucia Wetland Park is a unique multi-ecosystem encompassing virgin marine, coastal dune, wetland, estuarine, lake and bushveld ecologies. A large chunk of it contains Lake St Lucia, where hippopotamus and Nile crocodile are protected and huge numbers of waterfowl come to feed. Big-game fish and sharks prowl the St Lucia Estuary, and there are rich rewards for anglers. The best way to see it all is from the decks of the *Santa Lucia* on a boat tour. Part of the complex is the St Lucia Marine Reserve, stretching out to sea for 3km; no fishing of any kind is allowed here. The area has a variety of accommodation ranging from hotels and hutted camps to caravan parks and camp sites, and activities abound: deep-sea fishing, birdwatching, game-viewing, boating, walking, hiking ... The main centre, with many facilities, is St Lucia Resort.

Trips can be arranged to the Sodwana Bay National Park at the northernmost point of St Lucia Wetland Park. This cluster of lakes, connected to the sea by a stream known as Sodwana ('little one on its own'), is fringed by coastal dune forest and marshland, and the coral reefs – the world's most southerly – are a scuba diver's dream. Birdwatching, game-viewing and coastal game fishing are other major attractions. Accommodation varies from a comfortable lodge to log cabins and camp sites.

Greater St Lucia Wetland Park is 221km northeast of Durban (Natal Parks Board). St Lucia Publicity Association, PO Box 16, St Lucia 3936. Tel: 035–590 1339. Sodwana Bay National Park is about 400km from Durban (National Parks Board).

HLUHLUWE-UMFOLOZI GAME RESERVE

Hluhluwe (pronounced 'Shloo-shloo-way') and Umfolozi are two neighbouring

Hippos are protected in Lake St Lucia, and also thrive in the rivers of Kruger National Park

The conservation of the white rhino is a success story for Hluhluwe-Umfolozi Game Reserve

reserves (South Africa's oldest), linked by the Corridor Reserve and administered as a single unit. The total area of 96,000 hectares offers magnificent, diverse countryside ranging from woodland and forest to savannah and grassland. Umfolozi is associated with the square-lipped (white) rhino, which once faced extinction, and is famous for its rhino conservation programmes. It offers an impressive range of other animals including the Big Five (see page 22), cheetah and hippo. Together with Hluhluwe, the area sustains 84 mammal and 425 bird species. Game viewing is by autotrail, and there is hiking through Shaka's old hunting ground along the Wilderness Trails. Accommodation is in self-contained, self-catering cottages and huts ranging from basic to luxurious.
About 250km northeast of Durban (Natal Parks Board).

ITALA NATURE RESERVE

The best things about this 29,653-hectare reserve in the valley of the Pongola River are the conducted bushveld trails – three days long – during which hikers spend the night in tents. Itala's is a magnificent landscape of bushveld, deep valleys and cliffs and rivers for swimming. Its varied wildlife includes black and white rhino, giraffe, reedbuck, warthog and cheetah. There is excellent accommodation, as well as places to camp.
About 63km northeast of Vryheid (Natal Parks Board).

KOSI BAY NATURE RESERVE

Kosi Bay Nature Reserve is accessible only by four-wheeled drive vehicle. Hard by the Mozambique border, in a remote, flat, tree-covered, sandy region which once lay beneath the sea (hence the numerous shells found inland), it includes areas of mangrove swamp and marshes surrounding a system of lakes, and is a sanctuary for leatherback turtles, crocodiles, hippo, palm-nut vultures and fish eagles. Activities on offer include hiking trails, birdwatching and fishing, and the ocean is popular for scuba diving and spear fishing.
640km north of Durban. KwaZulu/Natal Department of Nature Conservation. Tel: 0331–946696.

Two of the Kruger's 8,000 elephants and (opposite, below) some of the myriad antelope

KRUGER NATIONAL PARK

For millennia great numbers of antelope, lion, elephant, giraffe and rhino have roamed in what is now the Kruger National Park, a vast game reserve covering nearly 20,000sq km of territory bordering Mozambique in the east and Zimbabwe in the north. Together with a number of private reserves on the west-central boundary of the Kruger (including Timbavati, Manyeleti, Sabi Sand, Londolozi and Mala Mala), this is South Africa's premier game reserve.

The park grew out of the amalgamation of the original Sabie Game Reserve and the Shingwedzi Reserve in 1903, and was named after President Paul Kruger, who already saw the need to preserve South Africa's wildlife heritage. Today the Kruger is busy with visitors, winter and summer. It has an extensive network of roads and a choice of routes, designated halts, view sites, picnic places, wilderness trails and numerous camps.

Habitat and wildlife

During winter, surface water is restricted to rivers and watering holes, where the animals congregate; the dry grass and almost leafless trees make for good visibility. In summer the park is transformed into a paradise of flowering trees and plants by the rains, and wildlife flourishes.

The southern section of the park, bordering on the Crocodile River, has mixed vegetation and is noted for its rarer mammals such as the roan, sable antelope and oribi. The southern central district is mopane veld (mopane is a tree evolved to withstand low rainfall), and the northern section – the best for birdwatchers – sandveld and lush riverine forests. Five rivers cross the park from west to east. Throughout, the Big Five (see page 22) are found in abundance, all but the leopard (of which there are around 90) easy to spot. There are about 1,500 lion, 8,000 elephant, over 25,000 buffalo, and a large number of endangered rhino, of both the black and white species. In all, the park sustains around 137 mammal species, including huge numbers of giraffe, zebra, impala and wildebeest; the rivers harbour hippo and crocodile. Here, too, is the world's highest density of birds of prey: look out for the Martial eagle and the lappet-faced vulture.

Getting there
The park has eight entrance gates easily accessible from Johannesburg, Durban and outlying towns. Skukuza, the Kruger's headquarters, has a host of tourist amenities, a supermarket and doctor's surgery, and an airstrip receiving charter flights from Johannesburg. Outside the park, Nelspruit (see page 88) and Phalaborwa have airports with regular scheduled flights from both Johannesburg and Durban.

Accommodation
More than 20 rest camps are dotted about the park, some luxurious, others basic, but generally of a high standard. All are fenced against the animals. Accommodation varies from fully equipped, air-conditioned, serviced chalets to huts with communal ablution and kitchen facilities. There are camp and caravan sites, and all the larger venues

Pretoriuskop National Lodge in the Kruger

have restaurants. Look carefully into the location of the camps in advance of your visit, so that you choose the best for your particular interest – birdwatching, perhaps, or viewing lion.

The private reserves at the edge of the Kruger have luxury game lodges with resident rangers. Wherever you stay, ask about guided night excursions, Landrover safaris and conservation-related events. Above all, book well in advance. Over 700,000 people visit the Kruger National Park each year.
Skukuza is about 500km northeast of Johannesburg. All enquiries and applications to the National Parks Board, PO Box 787, 0001 Pretoria. Tel: 012–343 1991. For information on the private reserves and their rest camps, see page 174.

The gun in front of the Town Hall bears witness to Ladysmith's violent history

a lych gate still bearing the scar of a shell from 'Silent Sue'. Guns used during the siege – the British Castor and Pollux and the Boers' Long Tom – stand in front of the Town Hall whose clocktower received the full impact of another Boer shell. The small Siege Museum, housed in the Market House turned siege ration post, details the story of the event. Mahatma Gandhi was here at the time – as a stretcher bearer; a statue of him adorns the gardens of the Hindu Vishnu Temple. Southwest of the town is the beautiful Muslim Soofie (Sufi) Mosque.

About 160km north of Pietermaritzburg. Siege Museum, Murchison Street. Tel: 0361–22231. Open: weekdays 8am–4.20pm, Saturday 8am–noon, Sunday 10–11.30am. Admission charge. Tourist information, Murchison Street. Tel: 0361–22992. For detailed information on the battle sites, enquire at the museum.

LADYSMITH

The pleasant Natal town of Ladysmith has a grim history. The Boers doggedly besieged it for 118 days (1899–1900) during the second Anglo-Boer War – their greatest mistake, according to General Jan Smuts (second premier of the South African Union), as it was tactically of minor importance and the delay here gave the British time to bring in many more troops. Every incident of the appalling ordeal, up to the heroic relief, was recorded in the British press. A few extant buildings witnessed the conflict. All Saints Anglican Church (begun 1882), for example, is entered via

LESOTHO

Lesotho, the mountainous kingdom of Moshoeshoe II, is a land roughly the size of Belgium landlocked within South Africa. As Basutoland it became independent from Britain in 1966. Desperately poor, its economy remains heavily reliant on international and South African aid and on exporting labourers to the South African goldmines.

In early times the San roamed the land, leaving many rock paintings. Nowadays the population is a mixture of mainly Sesotho-speakers. The Basotho (as the people are known) only emerged as a nation between 1815 and 1820, when Moshoeshoe the Great gathered the remnants of tribes scattered by the *Mfecane* (see box, page 9) and established a stronghold at Butha-Buthe. Later he moved to the mountain of Thaba-Bosiu near Maseru, the capital city. This 'Kingdom of the Sky' is famous today for its magnificent scenery, pony-trekking expeditions and the range of handicrafts made by its population, most of whom live in tiny mountain settlements. The archetypal Basotho is a horseman, multicoloured blanket on his shoulders, conical straw hat on his head, perhaps with a child riding on the croup of his saddle.

Maseru is 157km east of Bloemfontein.

LOUIS TRICHARDT AND AROUND

Northernmost Transvaal is dominated by the Soutpansberg (Salt Pan Mountain), haunt of the San until they were driven out by Venda tribes. In the southern foothills, Louis Trichardt, named after the Voortrekker who camped here in 1836, is the base from which to explore the region. Beyond the Soutpansberg, in a landscape dotted with mopani and baobab trees, is the intensely hot homeland of the Venda who settled here in the 18th century. They managed to avoid being overrun by settlers simply because the Soutpansberg was

impenetrable. In 1898, the Transvaal government gained control of the area and in 1979 it became the Venda independent 'homeland'. Many sites are sacred: at Dzata are ruins of ancient stone structures towards which the faces of dying Venda chiefs are turned; and down the Mutale River, Lake Fundudzi is home to the python god who once required annual human (female) sacrifice. The rites survive in a ceremony called the Domba, part of the puberty rites of young women.

Louis Trichardt is 378km northeast of Pretoria. The South African Tourism Board, PO Box 2814, Polokwane 0700. Tel: 0152–295 2829 or 3025.

Shepherd from Lesotho wearing the traditional blanket and straw hat

The drama of an African sunset in Mkuzi Game Reserve

MKUZI GAME RESERVE

Mkuzi Game Reserve is a magnificent small reserve established in 1912 in an area of fever trees and fossil remains, where once the Indian Ocean lapped the foothills of the Lebombo Mountains bordering Mozambique. It is a sanctuary for a variety of mammals including giraffe, black and white rhino, hippo and leopard. Some 413 bird species have also been recorded here. Four hides offer game-viewing during the dry season, and a bird observation platform overlooks Nsumu Pan. Accommodation is delightfully rustic. Day hikes can be arranged with a guide, and there is an autotrail. On the southeast border of Mkuzi is private Phinda Resource Reserve, with a habitat of immense diversity: sand forest, mountain grassland, tropical palm savannah, river forest and marshland. Phinda offers birdwatching, game-viewing, and luxurious accommodation.

About 355km northeast of Durban (Natal Parks Board). Phinda Resource Reserve is 3 hours from Durban.

NATAL MIDLANDS

Between the subtropical coastal belt and the Drakensberg (see pages 90–1), is a vast area of grassy plains and undulating farmland, the Natal Midlands. Here prize cattle and thoroughbred horses have replaced the herds of migrating game

Mkuzi offers some of South Africa's best game-viewing and birdwatching

which for centuries crossed this area, trailed by San hunters likewise escaping the cold winters of the high central plains. It attracted white settlers, causing bitter clashes with the then resident Zulus. Today it is popular for riding and trout fishing. An arts and crafts route linking artists' studios and workshops with hotels, country pubs, tea shops and health hydros is worth following. West of Pietermaritzburg (see page 102) are the spectacular 95m Howick Falls of the Mgeni River. To the west the Midmar Public Resort and Nature Reserve around the Midmar Dam offers watersports, riding, game-viewing and the Midmar Historical Village, an open-air museum. Outside Howick, the Game Valley Lodge contains lion, giraffe, hippo and white rhino (privately owned – reservations necessary). Mooi River, which has the biggest monthly livestock sale in southern Africa, is a pleasure and health resort with excellent sporting facilities.

Howick is 27km northwest of Pietermaritzburg. Howick–Mooi River (via Balgowan and Nottingham Road), 48km. Howick Publicity Association, Howick Falls. Tel: 0332–305305. Mooi River, Gateway Reservations and Real Estate cc, PO Box 174, Mooi River 3300. Tel: 0333–32450. Midmar Public Resort and Nature Reserve, and Game Valley Lodge, formerly Karkloof Nature Reserve (Natal Parks Board). Midmar Historical Village open: daily 9am–4pm. Admission charge.

NDUMO GAME RESERVE

This game reserve is often described as a miniature Okavango. Founded in 1924 on the floodplain of the Pongolo River, its rivers and shallow pans are teeming with wildlife – hippo and crocodile, aquatic birds and fish such as barbel,

tiger-fish, tilapia and bream. Many East African birds are found here – Ndumo appears to be the limit of their southern range. Here you might expect to see rollers, bee-eaters and nicators among other birds. In fact, there are over 400 species found in this area which is a paradise for serious birdwatchers.

Accommodation is in a hutted camp, but visitors must bring their own food. Near by, the Tembe Elephant Park is a new reserve created to protect the remnants of the huge Maputo elephants from the ravages of Mozambique's civil war. Accommodation is in an East African style tented camp.

Ndumo is about 470km northeast of Durban. KwaZulu Department of Nature Conservation. Tel: 0331–946696.

The impressive Howick Falls in the Mgeni River, west of Pietermaritzburg

THE TOWNSHIPS

Most of South Africa's towns and cities have, as 'satellites', one or more townships. These were the progeny of the Group Areas Act which separated South Africans according to the colour of their skin.

The most famous township is Soweto outside Johannesburg, but anyone who has kept abreast of postwar South African history will recognise the names of others: Alexandra, Boipatong, Crossroads, Katlehong, Langa, Tokoza, Tembisa ... These dusty, crime-ridden shanty towns are home to thousands of people, most of them living in shacks and all lacking an essential urban infrastructure. This legacy of apartheid has left the Government of National Unity with the formidable task of providing anew just about everything from housing to sanitation.

Soweto in many ways epitomises the concept 'township'. Historically, Johannesburg enticed itinerants in search of work, whatever their nationality. Many thousands of black Africans moved there from their traditional homes in the regions and from neighbouring southern African countries, and settled in camps around

Alexandra Township, near Johannesburg, and Cape Flats Township (top right) are typical poverty-stricken black shanty towns

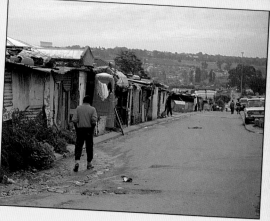

Many thousands of black South Africans have exchanged traditional rural life for life in the townships

the city perimeters. When these were closed down the inhabitants moved to Soweto (see page 133), with its rows of little tin-roofed houses a model township. Though Soweto had little heart to begin with, it was the source of much of the impetus for change in South Africa and became a byword for political violence. Today the situation is much more relaxed – indeed the arts are flourishing.

No visit to South Africa is complete without a visit to a township. Tours (never go alone or unaccompanied), providing opportunities to meet residents, help provide a balanced view of the New South Africa. Although anti-white militancy is still strong in the townships, a spirit of forgiveness is also abroad, and you will almost certainly come away marvelling at the dignity and patience of a people who, in the majority of cases, own absolutely nothing.

Victorian and proud of it: Pietermaritzburg City Hall

PIETERMARITZBURG

Pietermaritzburg, where cricket is played beside Alexandra Park's 19th-century Oval Pavilion, is one of the world's finest Victorian cities. The Voortrekkers established it in 1838 following their victory over Dingane at Blood River, and named it after two of their number, Piet Retief and Gerrit Maritz. The British took over in 1843, and Pietermaritzburg subsequently became capital of the Colony of Natal and seat of the region's government. Many of its buildings date from this period including the City Hall, a richly adorned specimen of colonial architecture, the Old Natal Parliament, Old Government House and Colonial Buildings.

In the Voortrekker Museum, housed in the small, gabled former Church of the Vow, is an ox-wagon and an ironwood chair said to have been Dingane's. The Natal Museum is devoted to the region's social and natural history, and the Macrorie House Museum, a restored mid-19th-century home, evokes early British settler lifestyle. In the Old Supreme Court (1871), the Tatham Art Gallery contains porcelain and glass as well as paintings. The Cathedral of St Peter (1872) is the burial place of Bishop John William Colenso (1814–83), heretic and founder of the Church of England in Natal. The city's thriving Indian population is architecturally represented by two Hindu temples, Sri Siva Soobramoniar and Mariammen Temple. *79km northwest of Durban.*
Pietermaritzburg Publicity Association, 177 Commerical Road. Tel: 0331–45 1348. Voortrekker Museum, 340 Church Street. Tel: 0331–946 834. Open: weekdays 9am–4pm, Saturday 8am–noon. Admission charge. Natal Museum, 237 Loop Street. Tel: 0331–451 404. Open: Monday to Saturday 9am–4.30pm, Sunday 2–5pm. Admission charge. Macrorie House Museum, 11 Loop Street. Tel: 0331–942

161. Open: Tuesday to Thursday
9am–1pm, Sunday 11am–4pm. Admission
charge. Tatham Art Gallery, corner of
Church Street and Commercial Road. Tel:
0331–421 804. Open: Tuesday to Sunday
10am–6pm.

SOUTH COAST

The most popular point south of Durban
is Amanzimtoti, a family resort with
summertime activities ranging from
beachside beauty contests to surf
lifesaving competitions. Going south,
Scottburgh offers safe bathing and Croc
World, where there's a wildlife museum,
snake pit and traditional Zulu
village, as well as crocodiles.
Kelso, Umdoni Park and
Pennington are small, peaceful
places which attract
caravanners and anglers. Ifafa
Beach has a fine lagoon for
skiing, canoeing and angling.

A little narrow-gauge
railway, the Banana Express
(see page 137) operates from
Port Shepstone, gateway to the
Oribi Gorge Nature Reserve, a
magnificent expanse of hills
and forest, home to, among
other creatures, vervet
monkeys and antelope. There
are 35km of walks and trails,
and a circular auto route through the
24km-long gorge. The Shell Museum at
Shelly Beach has South Africa's biggest
display of shells. The surfing at Lucien
Point and St Michael's is the best in the
area. Southbroom has excellent
windsurfing and boardsailing.
Port Shepstone is 128km southwest of
Durban, about 52km northeast of Port
Edward. Oribi Gorge Nature Reserve
(Natal Parks Board). Port Shepstone is
21km east of Kokstad (N2). Croc World,

MAHATMA GANDHI
A statue in Pietermaritzburg recalls an
incident in 1893 when Gandhi was
evicted from a first-class carriage at
Pietermaritzburg Station and sent to
the luggage wagon. Resisting, he was
thrown off the train. Later, at the height
of his prestige as the moral leader of
India, Mahatma Gandhi said that this
event was one of the most crucial in
his life because it triggered his
philosophy of peaceful resistance
based on the values of truth and
compassion.

Not every crocodile in Croc World is as
unmenacing as this baby

Old South Coast Road, Scottburgh. Tel:
0323–21103. Open: daily, 9am–5pm.
Feeding times: daily 11am and 3pm; also
daily exhibitions of Zulu dancing. Admission
charge. South Coast Publicity, PO Box
1253, Margate 4275. Tel: 03931–22322.
Shell Museum, Marine Drive, Shelly
Beach. Tel: 03931–75723. Open: in season,
daily 9am–5pm; out of season Wednesday to
Sunday, 10am–4pm. Admission charge.

'Roaring Monster', Sudwala Caves, in the Mankelekele massif of the Drakensberg

SUDWALA CAVES

West of Nelspruit (see page 88), on the slopes of the Mankelekele in the Drakensberg, are the awe-inspiring Sudwala Caves. Deep and labyrinthine, their limit is supposed to be 30km from the entrance – though only the first 2,500m have been penetrated (and only 600m are open to the public). Within are bizarre rock formations, spectacular stalactites and stalagmites, and strange fossils of prehistoric algae (stromatolites – the earliest identifiable forms of life). Although they have long provided a safe-haven for refugees, the caves were opened up only in 1964. They were last used as a refuge in the 19th century by the exiled Swazi regent, Somcuba; it was one of his officers, Sudwala, who showed the first Europeans into the caves. Below the entrance is a little resort with places to stay, swim and eat, and the open-air Owen's Museum contains life-size replicas of prehistoric creatures.

About 26km west of Nelspruit, on the R539.

Tel: 01311–64152. Open: daily. South African Tourism Board, Tarentaal Trading Post, corner of Kaapschehoop Road and N4 Highway, Nelspruit. Tel: 01311–44405.

SWAZILAND

The kingdom of Swaziland is sandwiched between South Africa and Mozambique. The kingdom goes back to the 18th century, when the Dlamini dynasty became established, but the country was only united in the mid-19th century by King Mswazi. Around this time Europeans were staking claims in Swazi territory, and from the 1870s British and Boer interests in the region increased and soon the Swazi kingdom had independence in name only. It became a British High Commission territory after the Anglo-Boer War, finally gaining independence in 1968.

Although only 364sq km in area, Swaziland has a variety of landscapes and habitats from rainforest to highveld and lowveld, and five main national parks and reserves. This is a beautiful country, unexpectedly sophisticated, and with a strong local culture. Mbabane, the capital city, is the best place to buy good handicrafts – woven grass bottles and mats, wooden objects, jewellery and pottery. Royal ritual is centred on Lobamba in the Ezulwini Valley. The airport is near the main commercial city, Manzini.

Mbabane is 361km east of Johannesburg. Ermelo to Mbabane, R65 via Nerston border point, or R39 via Oshoek border point.

TZANEEN AND AROUND

Amid tea plantations and subtropical vegetation, Tzaneen is an attractive little place producing cut flowers and fruit. There is plenty to see and do in the area. The Tzaneen Dam and Nature Reserve, with over 150 species of birds, offers watersports, picnicking and camping. There are several walks and forest drives from Duiwelskloof. To the east is the Modjadji Forest with a species of cycad, the Modjadji Palm (*Encephalartos transvenosus*), that evolved some 50 million years ago. Modjadji has a rain queen to whom people send gifts in the hope that she will make rain. The current incumbent is the direct descendant of a princess of the Karanga people of Zimbabwe who fled south in the 16th century, taking with her the rain-making secrets of the ruling family.

Further east, the Hans Merensky Nature Reserve was established in 1950 as a sanctuary for, among other animals, sable antelope, roan and zebra, and has a Tsonga kraal constructed as it may have looked a century ago.

Tzaneen is 67km west of Hans Merensky Nature Reserve. Soutpansberg Tourism Assocation, PO Box 1385, Louis Trichardt. Tel: 015539–720. Tzaneen Tourist Information, Town Clerk's Office, Agatha Street. Tel: 01523–71411. Tzaneen Dam and Nature Reserve, Sabie. Tel: 015303–5641. Hans Merensky Nature Reserve: take the R71 east of Tzaneen, then the R529 after 30km. Tel: 015238–635.

Tea plantations near Tzaneen. This region, with its high rainfall, is unusually fertile

Shaka's Way

Old Zululand covered a vast tract of central KwaZulu/Natal. The most interesting section lies north of Durban, particularly between the Tugela River and the Swazi border where there are Zulu homesteads, historic battlegrounds, memorials and forts. *Allow at least 2 days.*

Start at Stanger and drive up the N2 for 56km to Gingindlovu.

1 GINGINDLOVU

Gingindlovu ('swallower of the elephant') was the site of a military kraal built by Cetshwayo (Shaka's nephew) to commemorate victory over his brother, Mbulazi, in their

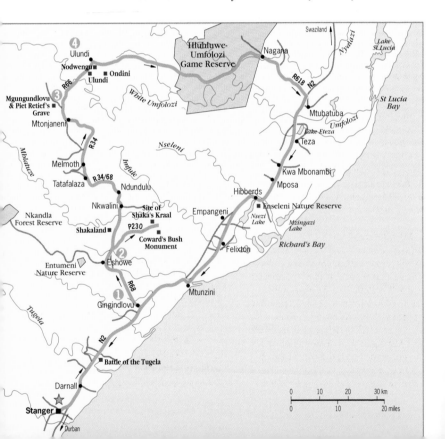

Statue of Voortrekker leader Piet
Retief in Pietermaritzburg

contest for the Zulu throne.
The kraal was destroyed by
the British in 1879.
*From Gingindlovu, take the
R68 to Eshowe (26km).*

2 ESHOWE

Eshowe ('sound of wind in
the trees') was a quiet
summer retreat for the
Zulus. Shaka's Kraal
overlooks the nearby
Nkwalini Valley.
Cetshwayo's first kraal was
here in 1860 before he
moved to Ulundi. It was
replaced by the British-built
Fort Nongqai (1883), now
the Zululand Historical
Museum. Near Eshowe
Nkandla Forest Reserve ('place of
exhaustion') is the grave of Cetshwayo
who died in 1884.
*For Shaka's Kraal, take the R68 north
from Eshowe (6km), turn right on the P230
(dirt road) for about 20km. Continue along
the R68 to Melmoth (27km), then turn on
to the R34 and continue for 24km to
Mgungundlovu.*

3 MGUNGUNDLOVU

Dingane moved the Zulu capital from
KwaDukuza to Mgungundlovu ('place of
the great elephant'), where Voortrekker
leader Piet Retief and his men were
executed in February 1838. Retribution
was grim: 3,000 warriors were killed at
the Battle of Blood River (see page 109).
The Mgungundlovu Museum occupies
the site of the kraal, the core of which
has been accurately rebuilt.
Take the R66 to Ulundi (about 18km).

4 ULUNDI

It was customary for a
newly crowned king to
establish his own capital;
Ulundi was Cetshwayo's
(1873). The British
destroyed it (1879), finally
breaking Zulu military
power. A second capital at
Ondini ('the heights'), was
burned by the Swazi. The
KwaZulu Monuments
Council rebuilt it as the
KwaZulu Cultural
Museum; the royal quarters
have been re-created. Close
to Ulundi, is the
Emakhosini Valley and
royal burial ground.
*From Ulundi, the route
branches east, passing through
the Hluhluwe-Umfolozi
Game Reserve (see page 92).
Leave the park on the R618 access road and,
at the junction with the N2, head south and
back via Stanger to Durban.*

Zululand Historical Museum,
Nongqai Road, Eshowe 3815. Tel:
0354–41141. Open: Monday to
Saturday 9am–4.30pm.
Mgungundlovu Museum, Private
Bag 831, Melmoth 3835. Tel:
03545–2254.
KwaZulu Cultural Museum, PO Box
523, Ulundi. Tel: 0358–791854.
Open: Monday to Friday,
9.30am–5pm.
Admission charge for all three
museums.
Tourist Information, Zululand Joint
Services Board, Private Bag X1025,
Richards Bay 3900. Tel: 0351–41404.

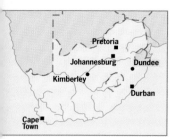

Natal Battlefields

Here Afrikaner settlers were confronted by the Zulu armies who later defeated even the might of Britain's Empire. And the Anglo-Boer War saw the Boers always outgunned, hopelessly outnumbered, and relentlessly pursued by massive columns. For them it was a long and depressing war of retreat. *Allow a leisurely weekend.*

Start at Dundee; the Talana Museum and battlefield lie just outside the town. Take the R33 for 5km.

1 TALANA BATTLEFIELD

This was the scene in 1899 of the first battle between British and Boers. The Boers won, then routed the British forces at Nicholson's Nek, after which the British withdrew to Ladysmith and the ensuing siege (see page 96). Situated on the battlefield is an impressive museum detailing the military history of the area and the history of Dundee – created in 1882 at the heart of newly located coalfields.

From Dundee to Isandhlwana it is about 80km on the R68; to Rorke's Drift, about 42km, also on the R68. Walk and tape tours are available for hire from the Talana Museum.

2 ISANDHLWANA AND RORKE'S DRIFT

On 22 January 1879, in the first major engagement of the Anglo-Zulu War, an unprepared British regiment was virtually annihilated by 25,000 Zulus. The *impi* (a group of armed warriors) rushed on to Rorke's Drift where, on 22 and 23 January 1879, 100 men won a 12-hour battle against overwhelming Zulu odds. A record number of 11 Victoria crosses were awarded. Like Isandhlwana, it is a sad site dotted with memorials. At Rorke's Drift there is good on-site interpretation, and a world-renowned Arts and Crafts centre.

Replica Voortrekker wagon on the site of the great Afrikaner victory at Blood River

Return to the R33. The turn-off is 27km from Dundee, and the Blood River monument 20km southeast of the R33.

3 BLOOD RIVER BATTLEFIELD

This event is one of the cornerstones of Afrikaner history. Avenging Dingane's murder of Piet Retief (see page 107), a small party of 464 Voortrekkers took on 12,000 Zulus (1838) – and won. They believed that God was on their side, and that theirs was a divine right to civilise southern Africa (see the Voortrekker Monument, page 133). Today the battlefield is a hallowed spot; on it is a replica *laager* of 64 wagons, reconstructed in bronze.

Returning to the R33, continue in the direction of Vryheid. After 15km, branch left onto the R34 and continue through Utrecht until the junction with the N11 (80km). Continue right, along the N11 to Volksrus.

4 MAJUBA BATTLEFIELD

On 27 February 1881 the Boers defeated the British army at Majuba Hill, bringing the First Anglo-Boer War to a close; 92 British soldiers were killed and 134 wounded. It resulted in the Boers regaining control of the South African Republic (Transvaal) and its capital, Pretoria. In the second Anglo-Boer conflict, after the Boers' stunning successes prior to their disastrous siege of Ladysmith, it was hoped that the British might abandon the war, mindful of the lessons of Majuba 18 years previously. *Return to Dundee via Newcastle (N11).*

Talana Museum, Private Bag 2024, Dundee 3000. Tel: 0341–22654. Open: weekdays 8am–4pm, Saturday 10am–4pm, Sunday noon–4pm. Admission charge. Tours of all the battlefields arranged by the museum.
Isandhlwana Battlefield – open: daily 8am–5pm. Admission charge.
Rorke's Drift – open: 8am–5pm. Craft Centre – open: weekdays 8am–4pm, Saturday 10am–3pm.
Blood River Battlefield – open: daily 8am–5pm.

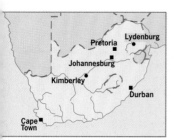

Drakensberg Panorama

The highlights of this Drakensberg route are natural, as opposed to man-made. It includes a series of magnificent views and incomparable scenery. *Allow a day.*

Start at Graskop, from which the scenic Panorama Route heads north along the edge of the escarpment on the R534 and R532 to the Blyde River Canyon.

1 GRASKOP

Graskop was once a major gold-mining settlement and is now a forestry centre. It is often known as 'Window of the Eastern Transvaal' due to its magnificent situation on the Drakensberg escarpment. Near by is an unforgettable viewing point, God's Window, which looks out over the Lowveld to the Kruger National Park. Just to the south of Graskop are the Mac-Mac Falls, twin waterfalls which plunge into the Mac-Mac River. A series of stepped natural pools on a tributary of this river were the scene of hectic gold-mining during the last century.

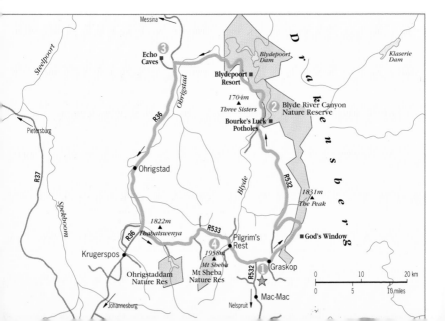

The stunning scenery of the Blyde River Canyon can be admired from viewing platforms

Beyond God's Window, the R532 continues on past the Bourke's Luck Potholes, which have been gouged into the rock by the powerful swirling action of the water, with their viewing platforms, to the Blydepoort Recreation Resort of the Blyde River Canyon and Nature Reserve.

2 BLYDE RIVER CANYON AND NATURE RESERVE

The wild Blyde River gouges its way down the Drakensberg through 1,000m in only 20km. In some places the canyon is over 700m deep. The scenery here is spectacular, with strategically placed viewing platforms allowing visitors to make best advantage of it. Dominating the area are peaks known as the Three Sisters (or Three Rondavels), which rise out of the mist. The nature reserve has hiking trails and bridle paths, and there are chalets, a caravan park and places to camp, swim and eat.

From the Blydepoort Recreation Resort, the R532 continues on to a junction. Take the R36. The Echo Caves turning is on the left.

3 ECHO CAVES

This sequence of natural chambers buried in the Molapong Valley yielded a rich hoard of Middle and Late Stone Age tools and implements. People lived here until comparatively recent times. The caves were opened to the public in 1924; if the stalactites within them are tapped, there is an echo effect from which the caves take their name. The so-called Museum of Man here has an open-air display of archaeological and palaeontological exhibits. There is also a motel and a caravan park near the caves.

Continue on the R36 through Ohrigstad, then turn left on to the R533 and follow the signs to Pilgrim's Rest.

4 PILGRIM'S REST

Pilgrim's Rest was the scene of lucrative gold workings in the 19th century. After 1873, when Alec Patterson first stumbled on the deposits, it had the reputation of being the richest alluvial deposit in southern Africa. A village developed which has survived almost in its entirety; today it is a 'living' museum. Old cottages have been preserved and the post office building houses memorabilia from the heady past of Pilgrim's Rest.

From Pilgrim's Rest, continue on the R533 to its junction with the R534 which leads back to Graskop.

Gauteng

*G*auteng is the smallest of South Africa's regions, but size is no indication of significance. Here lives the greatest concentration of South Africans. It is the powerhouse of South Africa and, by implication, of the whole of Southern Africa. Not for nothing did the region's old name, Pretoria Witwatersrand Vereeniging (PWV), become 'Gauteng' which, in Sotho, means 'place of gold'.

At the heart of Gauteng are two contrasting cities, Johannesburg and Pretoria, one ebullient and thrusting, the other quiet and dignified. Together with an almost endless agglomeration of townships, housing estates, suburbs and industries, they spread over the 80km rocky ridge, the Witwatersrand ('ridge of white waters'), a reef which happens to be a primary source of gold and uranium. The discovery of these riches just over a century ago changed the face of the Witwatersrand. Lush grassland is interspersed with huge mine dumps and strange lakes formed by water pumped from the mines.

High-profile Johannesburg overshadows its more staid neighbour, yet Pretoria is the country's administrative headquarters. Visitors generally spend more time in Johannesburg, but the surrounding regions – the Northwest, the Free State, the Northern Province and the Eastern Transvaal – are all easily accessible from both cities. Within Gauteng itself, the Magaliesberg Mountains provide welcome respite from city life, while the Sterk-fontein Caves are one of the world's most important prehistoric sites.

Left: bronze head of Paul Kruger, first president of the South African Republic, in Pretoria
Above right: Johannesburg Art Gallery

GAUTENG

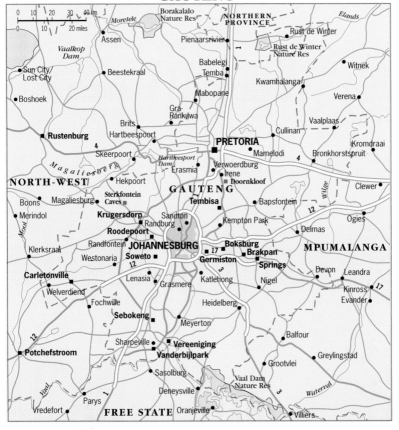

Johannesburg

Gold is the *raison d'être* of Johannesburg, the city otherwise known as Jo'burg, Joeys, or Egoli (City of Gold). Some of the world's deepest and richest goldmines are found here, and seven stock exchange listed mines are in and around Johannesburg. It is the source of 30 per cent of the world's gold.

Africa's wealthiest city was – and is – a boomtown, the continent's answer to Manhattan. It certainly looks like Manhattan: skyscrapers rise dramatically out of the veld, looking down on an urban sprawl afflicted with all the malaises of any American metropolitan jungle. Without Johannesburg – and gold – the Witwatersrand would be like the rest of the highveld: a region of maize fields and pastures.

Johannesburg has no obvious beauty to recommend it. Mine dumps litter the southern suburbs while the city centre is dominated by the cut and thrust of architecture designed to mirror the preoccupations of a community for which money, business and success are paramount. But Johannesburg is also a city of great poverty. Visit the townships and the gross inequalities engendered by apartheid are plain to see. It is a violent city, and can be dangerous. But it has an energetic, generous spirit that transcends racial strife and violence. Go down to the suburbs of Yeoville or Mellville, or the Market Precinct in the Newtown district, and there is an attractive street life that bubbles energetically.

The glittering night skyline of Johannesburg, a city built on gold

Johannesburg claims to be the cultural capital of the country. Certainly it is the centre of the film, music and media industries, and it has more theatres than any other city. It is rich in libraries, museums and galleries, several of which contain unique collections of local or indigenous art and artefacts. Cape Town also prides itself as the nation's cultural soul, but what Johannesburg has is its vast, vibrant satellite, Soweto, source of much of South Africa's creative wealth.

Johannesburg and Soweto, hand in hand, have acted, and still act, as the great social, political and economic forces shaping South African history.

You can escape the city centre bustle in Joubert Park, nearly as old as Johannesburg itself

BERNARD PRICE MUSEUM OF PALAEONTOLOGY

This is South Africa's premier museum wholly devoted to palaeontological research. It contains a vast hoard of fossils and a detailed collection of the bones and tools of *Australopithecus africanus* ('southern ape of Africa') – the possible ancestor of modern humans – who lived about three and a half million years ago. Discovered at the Sterkfontein Caves (see page 133) by Dr Robert Broom in 1936, *Australopithecus africanus* was about one metre tall. It may have walked upright, but its gait was awkward, with outsplayed feet – unlike its successor *Homo erectus* who lived about one million years ago (examples were excavated at Swartkrans, 1.6km from Sterkfontein) and walked much as we do now.
University of the Witwatersrand, Jorrison Street, Braamfontein. Tel: 011–716 1111.

CARLTON CENTRE

The 50-floor Carlton Centre is one of modern Johannesburg's most dominant landmarks – and an eyesore. But it has its

uses, containing a three-tier shopping centre, cinemas and exhibition space and, on the top floor, a viewing platform – the Carlton Panorama. On a clear day you can see as far as the Magaliesberg. The luxury Carlton Hotel adjoins the Centre.
Commissioner Street, entrance to Panorama at upper level, Carlton Shopping Centre. Tel: 011–331 6608. Open: daily 8am–11pm. Admission charge.

COMMERCIAL GALLERIES

Johannesburg art dealers have been instrumental in promoting fine art both locally and abroad. There is an abundance of mainstream and fringe galleries, as well as art centres, and a profusion of art workshops, foundations and centres provide education, hold exhibitions or sell the work of their artists'.

Of the commercial galleries, the Everard Read Contemporary Gallery, founded in 1912, is the oldest in the country, while the Goodman Gallery has promoted avant-garde work since the 1960s. The Newtown Galleries,

JOHANNESBURG

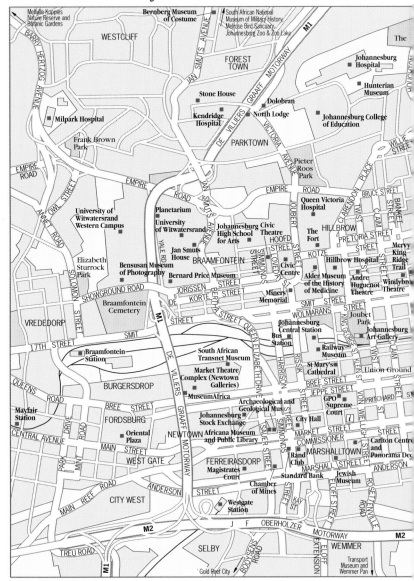

Melville Koppies
Nature Reserve and
Botanic Gardens

Bernberg Museum
of Costume

South African National
Museum of Military History,
Melrose Bird Sanctuary,
Johannesburg Zoo & Zoo Lake

M1

The

WESTCLIFF

FOREST
TOWN

Johannesburg
Hospital

Stone House

Dolobran

Hunterian
Museum

Milpark Hospital

Kendridge
Hospital

North Lodge

Johannesburg College
of Education

Frank Brown
Park

PARKTOWN

EMPIRE
ROAD

EMPIRE

Pieter
Roos
Park

EMPIRE   ROAD

Queen Victoria
Hospital

BRUCE STREET

University of
Witwatersrand
Western Campus

Planetarium

University
of Witwatersrand

Johannesburg Civic
High School   Theatre
for Arts

The
Fort

HILLBROW

PRETORIA STREET

Merry
King

Elizabeth
Sturrock
Park

Jan Smuts
House

BRAAMFONTEIN

HOOFD
KOTZE

Hillbrow Hospital

Ridge
Trail

Bensusan Museum
of Photography

Bernard Price Museum

Civic
Centre

Alder Museum
of the History
of Medicine

Andre
Huguenot
Theatre

Windybro
Theatre

Braamfontein
Cemetery

JORISSEN   STREET
DE KORTE STREET

Miners
Memorial

SMIT   STREET

Joubet
Park

VREDEDORP

SMIT

Johannesburg
Central Station

Johannesburg
Art Gallery

17TH STREET

Braamfontein
Station

Bus
Station

Railway
Museum

Braamfontein
Transnet Museum

South African
Transnet Museum

St Mary's
Cathedral

Union Ground

BURGERSDROP

Market Theatre/
Complex (Newtown
Galleries)

BREE STREET

JEPPE STREET

QUEENS   ROAD

MuseumAfrica

Archaeological and
Geological Mus

GPO
Supreme
Court

Mayfair
Station

BREE   STREET

FORDSBURG

Johannesburg
Stock Exchange

City Hall

Carlton Centre

CENTRAL AVENUE

Oriental
Plaza

MAIN   STREET

WEST GATE

Africana Museum
and Public Library

NEWTOWN

MARKET   STREET
COMMISSIONER
Rand
Club

MARSHALLTOWN

and
Panorama De

FERREIRASDORP

Magistrates
Court

MARSHALL   STREET
Standard Bank

Jewish
Museum

ANDERSON

Chamber
of Mines

MAIN REEF ROAD   ANDERSON   STREET

CITY WEST

Westgate
Station

M2

J F OBERHOLZER   MOTORWAY

M2

TREU ROAD

SELBY

WEMMER

Transport
Museum and
Wemmer Pan

Gold Reef City

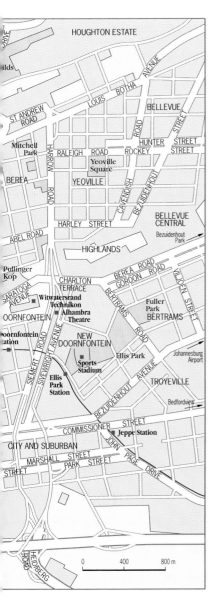

launched in 1991, is one of Johannesburg's most chic venues. Housed in a renovated warehouse in the Newtown Precinct, it provides exhibition space for South Africa's foremost artists, and hosts a number of exciting and unusual exhibitions combining the visual and performing arts. Of the non-commercial galleries, the Standard Bank Gallery, like the Civic Theatre Gallery, has continuous exhibitions. The Rembrandt van Rijn Gallery at the Market Theatre stages exhibitions at the cutting edge of contemporary art.

Everard Read Contemporary Gallery, 6 Jellicoe Avenue, Rosebank. Tel: 011–880 9419. Goodman Gallery, 3b Hyde Square, Jan Smuts Avenue, Hyde Park. Tel: 011–788 1113. Newtown Galleries, corner of Bree and Wolhuter streets. Tel: 011–838 1296. Standard Bank Gallery, corner of Commissioner, Fox and Harrison streets. Tel: 011–636 4231. Civic Theatre Galleries, Braamfontein. Tel: 011–403 3408. Rembrandt van Rijn Gallery, Market Theatre Complex, Wolhuter Street, Newtown Cultural Precinct. Tel: 011–832 1641. All galleries are open during shop hours.

DIAMOND CUTTING

How do you sort out the rubbish from the truly valuable? How do you know what to look for? A commercial company provides hour-long tours of diamond workshops, illustrating the sorting process and cutting and polishing. This is your chance to see a manufacturing jeweller at work – and a rare opportunity to purchase quality export diamonds and South African-designed gold.

Mynardts, 5 Simmonds Street. Tel: 011–334 8897. Reservations essential.

The Victorian General Post Office, one of the few old buildings left in Johannesburg

Beaux Arts, part Italianate in style. It has a stately interior suited to civic dignity. The building housing the Johannesburg Public Library dates from the 1930s. It once held the important Africana collections donated by Dr Gubbins, and the Geological Museum (both now relocated in the MuseumAfrica – see page 121).

Two of the most characterful early 20th-century Johannesburg buildings are the Standard Bank (see page 123) and the Rand Club with its Rhodes associations (see page 123). The office block known as the Corner House is South Africa's first-ever skyscraper. Built in 1903, it was a monument to the prosperity of the young city, and was said 'to glitter in the afternoon sun'. With its curious mix of styles – classical jostling with Arts and Crafts and Art Nouveau – it set the style for subsequent early 20th-century Johannesburg buildings.

General Post Office, Rissik Street. Tel: 011–422 2030. City Hall, corner of Market, Rissik, President and Harrison streets. Tel: 011–491 8911. Johannesburg Public Library, Market Square. Tel: 011–836 3787. The Corner House, corner of Commissioner and Simmonds streets.

EARLY JOHANNESBURG

Mining and commerce have produced some of Johannesburg's finest buildings. However, as the city grew, successive generations destroyed its predecessors's buildings. Today you must look hard to find anything over 20 years old.

The General Post Office (1896) is primarily a republican building, its clock tower added after the Anglo-Boer War by Lord Milner to commemorate the coronation of King Edward V11 in 1902. The lavishly ornamented interior is intact and is well worth a visit. The City Hall is a rather unwieldy post-Union edifice, part

JEWISH MUSEUM

The museum outlines the history of South African Judaism from the 1920s to the present. South Africa, and Johannesburg in particular, has a large Jewish community many of whom arrived in the 1920s.

Sheffield House, corner of Kruis and Main streets. Tel: 011–331 0331. Open: Monday to Thursday 9am–1pm, 2–5pm. Admission charge.

The Johannesburg Art Gallery has an eclectic mix of European and African art

JOHANNESBURG ART GALLERY

This contains a mixed collection, with works by El Greco, Picasso (notably a *Harlequin*) and Rodin displayed alongside others by locals such as Jackson Hlungwane and William Kentridge. The origins of the collection derive from the sale in London of a 21½-carat diamond ring owned by Lady Phillips, wife of 'Randlord' Sir Lionel Phillips. With the proceeds she bought three paintings by the English Impressionist Philip Wilson Steer, and then persuaded mining magnates Max Michaelis, Otto Beit, Abe Bailey, Julius Wernher and Frederick Ekstein to contribute funds towards the founding of an art gallery for the city for which Sir Edwin Lutyens would prepare a design.

The foundation stone was laid in 1911, and a grand building in the classical manner followed. It was extended in 1984 and today houses not only the European collections, but also the Brenthurst Collection of African Art – a diverse array of 'curiosities' which left South Africa in the hands of missionaries, travellers and scientists returning to Europe

> ### GOLDMINES
> It would be a wasted opportunity not to visit a working goldmine. The problem is that the mines themselves are not terribly keen on having you there. Nonetheless, persevere – it really is worth it. Tours are spasmodic, and are organised by the Chamber of Mines. *Chamber of Mines, Holland Street. Tel: 011–838 8211. Admission charge. Advance booking essential. Conducted tours Tuesday to Thursday.*

in the 19th century. Most of the pieces are of Nguni, Sotho or East African origin; the oldest ones date from the mid-19th century. The collection provides important evidence of indigenous cultural tradition in Southern Africa.

The complex has an excellent coffee shop and a gift shop stocked with crafts such as Ndebele beadwork and colourful local ceramics.

Joubert Park. Tel: 011–725 3130/3180. Open: Tuesday to Sunday 10am–5pm. Free.

Enigmatic African woodcarving, Johannesburg Art Gallery

Market Theatre Precinct, a civilised place to relax in an exhausting city

JOHANNESBURG STOCK EXCHANGE

Though not South Africa's original stock exchange, this was the first to deal in gold stocks (1887). The early building was too small for all the activity, and it was allowed to spill out into the street. An area between Commissioner and Market streets was sealed from the traffic with chains – hence the expression 'between the chains' which became the international jargon for stock trading. The modern stock exchange deals in gold as well as all other shares.
Corner of Diagonal and Pritchard streets. Tel: 011–833 6580. Guided tours: weekdays at 11am. Free.

JOHANNESBURG ZOO AND ZOO LAKE

Situated in Herman Eckstein Park, the zoo holds some 300 different species of animals – many threatened with extinction. Its objectives have evolved from being purely recreational: now it incorporates educational, conservation and research functions. Near by, the Zoo Lake area is well frequented at weekends. You can take a boat trip on the water, or view the monthly open-air Art in the Park exhibition.
Jan Smuts Avenue, Parktown. Tel: 011–646 2000. Open daily 8.30am–5.30pm. Admission charge.

MARKET THEATRE PRECINCT

This area, adjacent to the MuseumAfrica complex, is one of the most enjoyable places to spend time during the day in this vast, sprawling city. In and around refurbished turn-of-the-century Indian and citrus-fruit market warehouses are four theatres, an art gallery, shops and places to eat, drink and listen to music. It is also the scene of a lively Saturday market (see page 145). The Market Theatre itself (see page 147) is housed in the grandest of the market buildings. Built in 1911, its typically Beaux-Arts

MuseumAfrica, an ambitious multicultural and multifunctional complex

frontage disguises the utilitarian wood, glass and iron railway shed type market hall. That it survived to be restored and reused was a major breakthrough for the conservation of early urban Johannesburg. A landmark in the fight against apartheid, it is internationally renowned. Luminaries in its past and present include director-actor Athol Fugard, and actors John Kani, Barney Simon, Janet Suzman and Anthony Sher. *Newtown Cultural Precinct, Bree Street. Tel: 011–832 1641.*

MUSEUMAFRICA

Housed in an old market warehouse in the heart of the city's Newtown Cultural Precinct, the MuseumAfrica comprises a variety of older museums once dispersed around the city. Opened in 1994, it aims to reach all areas of the diverse community and promotes unity and reconciliation through education. It also accommodates diverse activities, such as music, dance, praise (through music, dance and lyrics) and story-telling, as an essential resource for education.

The original Africana Museum (founded in 1934) documents paintings, geological specimens, prints, photographs and objects relating to the history of a vast area – stretching from the Cape to the Zambezi. It contains a comprehensive collection of art from all groups of South Africa's population. The Geological Museum illustrates the geological history of the earth. The Bensusan Museum of Photography contains hundreds of photographs, including classics by pioneers such as Fox-Talbot, daguerreotypes, collotypes, magic lanterns and early cinematographic equipment. Collected by Dr A D and Mrs Bensusan and presented to the city, it is one of the most envied collections of its kind in the world.

MuseumAfrica also houses the Museum of South African Rock Art, the Camera Obscura, the Cultural History Museum Collection and a variety of other special collections. This is a heroic effort to tell the story of South Africa from the Stone Age to the Nuclear Age with as much objectivity as possible. *121 Bree Street. Tel: 011–833 5624. Open: Tuesday to Sunday 9am–5pm. Admission charge.*

ORIENTAL PLAZA

Situated in the Fordsburg district, for many years the Indian area, Oriental Plaza is close to the Market Theatre Precinct and illustrates yet another facet of this city's great cultural diversity. In the 1970s, in line with the Group Areas Act, many of the district's buildings were razed to the ground, and the Indian community moved out to Lenasia township. The authorities then built Oriental Plaza to replace the tiny shops, and this is now a lively commercial market area with all the hustle and bustle of India – the smell of spices, curry houses and Indian takeaways, bright fabrics, exotica, pets, kitchen equipment and brass.
Between Main and Bree streets. Tel: 011–838 6752.

PARKTOWN

This Johannesburg neighbourhood was South Africa's pioneer garden suburb. The architect Sir Herbert Baker's home, Stone House, is here, and also Moot Cottage, headquarters of Lord Alfred Milner (British High Commissioner for southern Africa from 1897) and his 'kindergarten', a team of young Englishmen brought over to administer the Transvaal after the Peace of Vereeniging. The Parktown and Westcliff Heritage Trust organises tours around the area – including visits to some of the more important buildings – on its Randlords Heritage Walk.
Parktown and Westcliff Heritage Trust. Tel: 011–482 3349, mornings only.

PLANETARIUM

Discover the secrets of the southern skies at the Planetarium located on the campus of the University of the Witwatersrand. Much of the splendour of the night sky is lost to Europeans and North Americans

Stone House, Parktown, former home of the architect Sir Herbert Baker

because so much artificial light is allowed to spill into it. This is not the case in southern Africa – yet. Even without the Planetarium to guide you through it, the night display seen with the naked eye is hugely rewarding. The Planetarium's fascinating programmes frequently change, and there is an excellent bookshop selling maps and charts.
Yale Road, Milner Park. Tel: 011–716 3199. Reservations essential.

RAND CLUB
The Rand Club is Johannesburg's answer – right down to the all-male anachronistic preserves within – to the gentlemen's clubs of London's Pall Mall. All leather and silence, it was built in 1904 by the mining magnates, who saw themselves as an aristocracy among English-speaking South Africans, as a place where they could gather alone without blacks and Boers and Jews. Cecil John Rhodes's boyish face still stares down from the wall: he was one of the directors of the original club, a primitive hut facing the street at this same location. Today's huge and magnificent French Renaissance-style building is a far cry from those early days.
Corner of Loveday, Commissioner and Fox streets. Tel: 011–834 8311.

SOUTH AFRICAN NATIONAL MUSEUM OF MILITARY HISTORY
This, one of Johannesburg's most popular museums (formerly the War Museum), is located in the Herman Eckstein Park. On display are fighter aircraft from both world wars, weapons, uniforms, flags and other wartime equipment – including a German one-man submarine.
Herman Eckstein Park (Johannesburg Zoo), Saxonwold. Tel: 011–646 5513. Open: daily 9am–4.30pm. Admission charge.

The impressive entrance to the Rand Club, built strictly for English gentlemen

SOUTH AFRICAN TRANSNET MUSEUM
The Transnet Museum houses old steam locomotives, a unique collection of model trains, and reflects all aspects of the South African Transport Services.
Johannesburg Station Complex. Tel: 011–773 9118. Open: weekdays 7.30am–3.45pm. Admission charge.

STANDARD BANK
At the turn of the century, the Standard Bank was considered the ideal of what a bank should look like. Part stone, part brick, steel-framed but covered in Renaissance clothing, it was, according to one newspaper, 'very bold and striking ... absolutely the finest premises devoted to banking in South Africa'. Today it still holds its own among the skyscrapers abutting it. It was completed in 1907 – building work having been held up because all stocks of steel had been diverted to San Francisco for rebuilding after the earthquake.
Corner of Commissioner, Fox and Harrison streets. Tel: 011–636 9112.

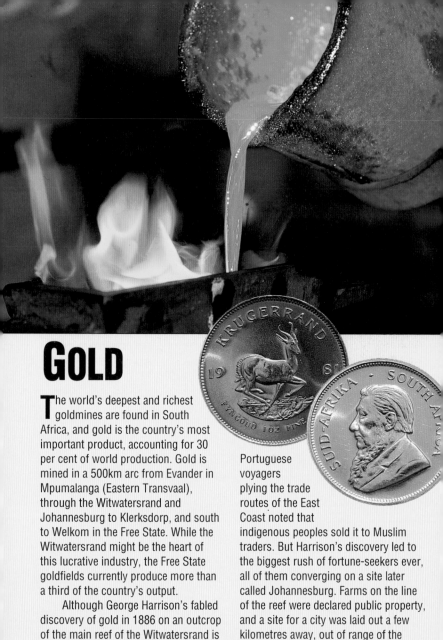

GOLD

The world's deepest and richest goldmines are found in South Africa, and gold is the country's most important product, accounting for 30 per cent of world production. Gold is mined in a 500km arc from Evander in Mpumalanga (Eastern Transvaal), through the Witwatersrand and Johannesburg to Klerksdorp, and south to Welkom in the Free State. While the Witwatersrand might be the heart of this lucrative industry, the Free State goldfields currently produce more than a third of the country's output.

Although George Harrison's fabled discovery of gold in 1886 on an outcrop of the main reef of the Witwatersrand is well documented, it was not the earliest gold mined in South Africa. Early Portuguese voyagers plying the trade routes of the East Coast noted that indigenous peoples sold it to Muslim traders. But Harrison's discovery led to the biggest rush of fortune-seekers ever, all of them converging on a site later called Johannesburg. Farms on the line of the reef were declared public property, and a site for a city was laid out a few kilometres away, out of range of the workings. This was a latterday El Dorado, and there was huge competition for

Pouring a gold bar (opposite page); both sides of a krugerrand (inset); mining in Johannesburg (left); a gold bullion bar (below)

countries work the mines. Virtually all are black, and a common *lingua franca, Fanakalo* (incorporating Afrikaans, English and Zulu), has developed, enabling them to communicate. Although goldmining is no longer undertaken within the Johannesburg city area, the wealth it engendered looks here to stay, and the pursuit of riches still drives many of the inhabitants of this 'city of gold'.

concessions. Diamond millionaires from Kimberley became gold magnates too, presiding over some of the richest and most profitable mines ever. The existence of such treasure led to political upheaval, petty wars with the earlier inhabitants of the area and, ultimately, the Anglo-Boer Wars.

Today, over half a million men from more than 10 Southern African

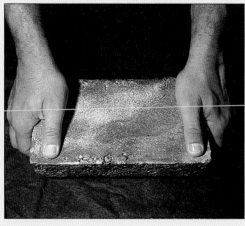

Pretoria

*P*retoria has nothing like the street culture so prevalent in Johannesburg – and nothing like its neighbour's violence. In fact it is rather a dull place; ask any South African. They regard it as a slow, provincial capital, a bastion of Afrikanerdom and pious conservatism – which would be true if there wasn't an undercurrent of gaiety which flouted all the rules. Even keen nightclubbing Johannesburgers often trek out to Pretoria to trawl the bars and nightspots.

The Raadsaal (Parliament), built in the 1890s as Kruger's powerhouse

Natural History and Cultural History museums are second to none. Then there is the Voortrekker Monument. The subject of much derision over the years from liberals frustrated by the, to them, incomprehensible logic of the apartheid rationale, it is in fact a poignant monument to a people who truly believed that theirs was a God-given right to oppress another race, with tragic consequences. White elephant, folly, object of shame – whatever one might call it, it is worth a look.

Pretoria is home to foreign embassies and much of the upper echelons of the country's military. It is the country's administrative HQ, and the nabobs in charge have their offices in the Union Buildings which stare out over the city from the Acropolis-like Meintjieskop when they are not sitting in Parliament in Cape Town. The violence that has afflicted nearly all of South Africa's other major cities, apart from the ANC car-bomb which killed 19 people in 1983, has largely passed Pretoria by.

This is also a city of learning. Pretoria University has an excellent reputation, the world's largest correspondence university, UNISA, is here, and the

No visit to Gauteng would be complete without a sojourn, no matter how brief, in Pretoria. Sitting at the highest point of the highveld, prosperous and within easy reach of the wilder, more rugged areas of the Northern Province and Eastern Transvaal regions, it is a handsome, spacious place, noted for its gardens and the battalions of civil servants who wander its streets at lunchtime.

PRETORIA

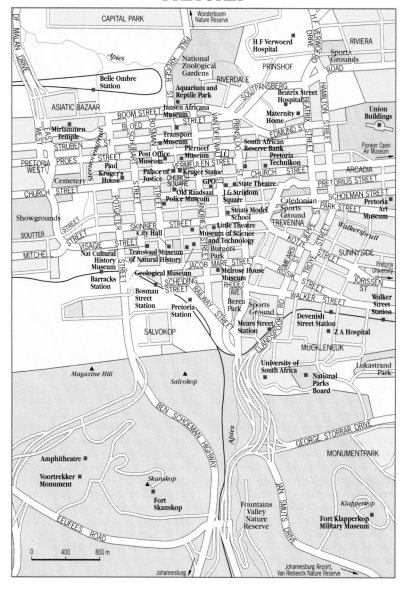

CAPITAL PARK

Wonderboom
Nature Reserve

H F Verwoerd
Hospital

RIVIERA

Sports
Grounds

DF MALAN DRIVE

PAUL KRUGER STREET

H F VERWOERD DRIVE

HAMILTON STREET

Apies

National
Zoological
Gardens

PRINSHOF

ROAD

Belle Ombre
Station

RIVERDALE

SOUTPANSBERG

Beatrix Street
Hospital

BEATRIX STREET

Union
Buildings

ASIATIC BAZAAR

Aquarium and
Reptile Park

Jansen Africana
Museum

Maternity
Home

Pioneer Open
Air Museum

BOOM STREET

BLOED

VAN DER WALT

EDMUND ST

Mirlammen
Temple

BOSMAN

Transport
Museum

PRINSLOO

South African
Reserve Bank

ARCADIA

STRUBEN

SCHUBART

Plierneef
Museum

Pretoria
Technikon

PROES

Post Office
Museum

VERMEULEN STREET

CHURCH   STREET

Steenhovenspruit

PRETORIA
WEST

Paul
Kruger's
House

Palace of
Justice

Kruger Statue
CHURCH
SQUARE

PRETORIUS STREET

Cemetery

GPO

State Theatre

SCHOEMAN STREET

Pretoria
Art
Museum

CHURCH   STREET

POTGIETER

Old Raadsaal
Police Museum

I G Strijdom
Square

PARK STREET

Showgrounds

STREET

Stoats Model
School

Caledonian
Sports
Ground

Walkerspruit

SOUTTER

SKINNER   STREET

ANDRIES

Little Theatre

TREVENNA

KOTZE

JEPPE

TROYE

SUNNYSIDE

MITCHELL

City Hall

Museum of Science
and Technology

Burgers
Park

MEARS

Pretoria
University

Nat Cultural
History
Museum

VISAGIE   STREET

Transvaal Museum
of Natural History

JACOB

MARE STREET

RISSIK

JORISSEN
ST

Barracks
Station

STREET

Geological Museum

SCHEIDING

Melrose House
Museum

WALKER   STREET

Walker
Street
Station

Bosman
Street
Station

RAILWAY STREET

RHODES
AVE

Berea
Park

Pretoria
Station

Sports
Ground

Devenish
Street Station

SALVOKOP

Mears Street
Station

ELANDSPOORT RD

Z A Hospital

MUCKLENEUK

Magazine Hill

Salvokop

University of
South Africa

National
Parks
Board

Lukastrand
Park

BEN SCHOEMAN HIGHWAY

Apies

GEORGE STORRAR DRIVE

MONUMENTPARK

Amphitheatre

Voortrekker
Monument

Skanskop

JAN SMUTS DRIVE

Klapperkop

Fort
Skanskop

Fountains
Valley
Nature
Reserve

Fort Klapperkop
Military Museum

EEUFEES   ROAD

0   400   800 m

Johannesburg

Johannesburg Airport,
Van Riebeeck Nature Reserve

You can't miss the statue of Paul Kruger, gazing out over Church Square

CHURCH SQUARE AND CHURCH STREET

Church Square was the hub of early Pretoria. Here ox-wagons from the country were outspanned (unyoked), and here the city's first shops opened. Much of it has been spared the developer's bulldozer, and today it is a handsome urban space which parades the evolving styles of South African architecture. Anton van Wouw's statue of Paul Kruger dominates the square. The Raadsaal (begun 1889), the seat of Kruger's republican government built using funds from the newly established gold fields, is the architectural prototype of many buildings of its epoch – notably Berlin's Reichstag. Opposite is the Palace of Justice, completed after the Anglo-Boer War. Its interior, like the Raadsaal's, is dripping with lavish cut stone, brass, stained glass and tiles. The headquarters of the South African Reserve Bank was designed by Sir Herbert Baker with a flanking loggia set on a high rusticated base that reappears on Baker's Union Buildings (see page 131).

Church Street, traversing the square from east to west, connects central Pretoria with the countryside beyond. As it crosses the Apies River, just to the east of Church Square, it is adorned with carved lions presented to Kruger by 'Randlord' Barney Barnato. Going east it enters the suburb of Arcadia, dominated by the rocky outcrop, Meintjieskop, site of the Union Buildings. Going west it leads to the Hartbeespoort Dam.
Pretoria Publicity Association, Ground Floor, Munitoria Building, corner of Prinsloo and Vermeulen streets. Tel: 012–323 1430 or 1432. For guided tours of the square – tel: 012–814 911 or 012–201 3223.

JANSEN AFRICANA MUSEUM

This interesting small museum exhibits silver, porcelain, Dutch ceramics and art.

*Struben Street. Tel: 021–420 9111. Open:
Monday to Friday 8am–4pm. Admission
charge.*

MELROSE HOUSE

Melrose House is a monument to 19th-
century magnate George Heys, who
made a fortune as the principal operator
of stage-coaches and transport vehicles in
the Transvaal. Built in 1886, the red-
roofed house sprawls hideously amid
lush gardens, an extravaganza of gables
and turrets, curlicues and right angles,
rustication, wrought iron and white
stucco. Heys' original furnishings are
still *in situ* and, there is a collection of
19th-century furniture showing English
influence.

In 1902 Melrose House was
requisitioned by the British and occupied
by Lord Roberts, then Lord Kitchener.
It was here that the Treaty of
Vereeniging was signed, in May 1902,
bringing the second Anglo-Boer War
to a close.
*275 Jacob Mare Street. Tel: 012–328 3265.
Open: Tuesday to Saturday 10am–5pm
(Thursday 8pm), Sunday noon–5pm.
Admission charge.*

NATIONAL CULTURAL HISTORY
MUSEUM

This fine museum is dedicated to the
study of South Africa's various
population groups, and looks at their
domestic utensils, furnishings and
applied arts. Its collection of South
African silver is excellent, so is its array
of San rock art.
*Boom Street. Tel: 012–323 3128. Open:
Monday to Friday 8am–4pm. Admission
charge.*

NATIONAL ZOOLOGICAL
GARDENS

If you cannot get to a game reserve, head
for Africa's best zoo. The Pretoria Zoo
contains a comprehensive collection of
indigenous and foreign species housed in
semi-natural surroundings. There are
more than 3,500 animals, some of which,
like the pygmy hippo, black-faced impala
and brown hyena, are extremely rare. A
cable car ascends to the local *koppie* – the
ride gives you a great view over the
animals' habitat. There is also an
aquarium and reptile park. The zoo is set
in gardens and has places to eat and
drink.
*Corner of Boom and Paul Kruger streets.
Tel: 012–328 3265. Open: daily 8am–5pm.
Admission charge.*

Not quite the savannah, but Pretoria Zoo is
home to zebra and many other species

PAUL KRUGER'S HOUSE

On Kerk (Church) Street, opposite the Dutch Reformed Church where he preached and worshipped, is the little white-stuccoed, tin-roofed home of Paul Kruger, President of the old South African Republic. This simple dwelling typifies Kruger, a man of deep piety and stubborn principle, the archetypal Boer, who believed the earth was flat and the 'old people' of the Trek were indeed God's Elect. He lived here from 1883 to 1900 before going into exile in Switzerland where he died in 1904. Like Smuts's home at Doornkloof (see page 132), it is a shrine to the memory of one of the country's most remarkable public figures.

Kerk (Church) Street. Open: Monday to Saturday 8.30am–4pm, Sunday 11am–4pm. Admission charge.

You can visit President Kruger's humble home in Pretoria's Church Street

PRETORIA ART MUSEUM

A small but important collection includes works by major South African artists Pierneef, Maggie Laubscher, Anton van Wouw and Irma Stern. The international collection is largely of Dutch and Flemish art and includes works by Frans Hals and Van Dyck.

Corner of Schoeman and Wessels streets, Arcadia Park. Tel: 021–344 1807. Open: weekdays 9am–4.30pm. Admission charge.

TRANSVAAL MUSEUM OF NATURAL HISTORY

Founded in 1893, the museum is devoted to the study of natural history and ethnography. It is particularly good on birdlife; the Austin Roberts Bird Hall contains the most comprehensive collection of birds south of the equator. Roberts compiled the authoritative *Birds of South Africa*, the standard work on the subject, and every example is here, numbered and accompanied by a recording of its sound. Here too are mammals, reptiles, shells and a skeleton of the extinct dodo. The museum has an excellent bookshop with a wide variety of natural history publications.

The adjoining Museum of Geological Survey houses a display of the earth's geology and mineralogy, with the emphasis on South Africa – where the Transvaal region with its deep treasure of valuable rocks, minerals, metals and precious stones is one of the richest geological storehouses on earth.

Paul Kruger Street. Tel: 012–322 7632. Open: Monday to Saturday 9am–5pm, Sunday 11am–5pm. Admission charge.

The imposing Union Buildings, present-day headquarters of South Africa's government

UNION BUILDINGS

Images of the Union Buildings were beamed around the world in April 1994, when Nelson Mandela was sworn in as the country's first black president in the amphitheatre at the building's centre, where Dr Verwoerd's funeral service was held nearly 30 years before. Since the complex was completed in 1913, it has served as the headquarters of the South African government, and here President Mandela now has his office.

Between 1910 and 1912, Sir Herbert Baker built two great sandstone blocks of official buildings in a classical style, a linking curved amphitheatre between them. Columned loggias were intended by Baker to lure the ministers from their offices so that they could 'lift up their eyes to the high veld'. Monumental and imposing, it was at the time imbued with great symbolism: the twin-domed towers were to represent the English and Afrikaans peoples, a reconciliation between Briton and Boer as signified by the 1910 Act of Union. The curved colonnade linked them, hand in hand. None of this symbolism made room for South Africa's black population. They were included in Baker's plan only by a scheme for a 'small partly open Council Place for Native Indabas (meetings), where, without coming into the Building, Natives may feel the majesty of Government'. But that was never built. After the success of this project, Baker went on to collaborate with Lutyens in New Delhi, India.

Open: office hours. Tours can be arranged (tel: 012–325 2000).

Johannesburg and Pretoria Environs

CULLINAN

Here in 1905 Thomas Cullinan found the world's largest diamond – the 3,106-carat 'Cullinan' which the Transvaal Government presented to King Edward VII. The Premier Diamond Mine was established and the mining village of Cullinan grew up around it. Tours are available.

Premier Diamond Mine, 95 Oak Avenue, Cullinan. 40km east of Pretoria. Tel: 012–134 0081. Open: Monday to Saturday 10.30am. Booking essential. Admission charge.

DOORNKLOOF – GENERAL SMUTS'S HOUSE

A modest galvanised iron and wood house on the farm Doornkloof was the home of statesman General Jan Smuts

until his death in 1950. It contains original furnishings and memorabilia – including two of his cars.

Take the N1, going south from Pretoria to Irene. Tel: 012–667 11766. Open: weekdays 9.30am–1pm, 1.30–4.30pm. Open until 5pm weekends. Admission charge.

GOLD REEF CITY

Gold Reef City, built around a famous goldmine, is a reconstruction of pioneer Johannesburg during the gold rush. There's a Victorian funfair, brewery, pubs, hotel, restaurants, apothecary, Chinese laundry, tailor and newspaper office. See tribal dancing by the 16-member Gold Reef City International Dancers team, and visit No 14 shaft, once the world's richest gold mine.

9km south of Johannesburg, just off the N1. Tel: 011–496 1600. Open: Tuesday to Sunday 9.30am–11pm. Admission charge. Newspaper listings detail special events.

Colourful tribal dance performance at Gold Reef City, near Johannesburg

MAGALIESBERG

The Magaliesberg mountains stretch about 120km from a point west of Rustenburg in the Northwest to east of Pretoria. They offer unlimited walks, swimming in mountain pools, climbing, birdwatching and picnicking, as well as angling and boating at Hartbeespoort Dam. Hotels, guest houses, camp sites and caravan parks abound.
Hartbeespoort Dam is about 35km west of Pretoria.

SOWETO

Soweto is the largest black city south of the equator. An amalgamation of dormitory townships – its name is short for South Western Townships – it was at the forefront of the black liberation struggle. Today this bubbling city is expanding so fast that it threatens to overshadow its parent, Johannesburg. Home to more than 2.5 million people, it suffers inadequate facilities and bizarre inequalities: mansions and miserable cardboard shacks; BMWs and horse-drawn carts. Orlando Stadium is the best football ground in South Africa, but there are only two cinemas. Despite such deprivation, creativity seethes in Soweto, which counts some of the country's leading musicians and singers, painters and poets among its citizens. See also pages 100–1.
Soweto lies about 10km south of Johannesburg. For guided tours: Soweto Tours, tel: 011–932 000 or 932 3536; Jimmy's Face to Face, tel: 011–331 6109.

STERKFONTEIN CAVES

The caves, discovered in 1896, are one of the world's major prehistoric sites. In 1936 Dr Robert Broom found, exposed after its 2.5-million-year interment, the first adult cranium of *Australopithecus*

The huge Voortrekker Monument, symbol of Afrikaner nationalism, arouses mixed feelings

africanus, hailed as the 'missing link' between ape and man. Today you see six cathedral-like chambers, an underground lake, and a museum containing fossils found in the caves.
Take the R563 Hekpoort Krondraai Road from Krugersdorp, northeast of Johannesburg. Tel: 011–956 6342. Open: daily except Monday, 9am–4pm. Admission charge.

VOORTREKKER MONUMENT

This great, granite block (built in the 1940s) was designed to symbolise the indomitable spirit of the Voortrekkers. The lower hall contains the inscription 'Ons vir jou, Suid Afrika' ('We for thee, South Africa'). Precisely at noon on 16 December – the anniversary of the Battle of Blood River – a shaft of sunlight reveals it, together with a tableau depicting Voortrekkers making a vow to God to build a church if He should grant them victory over the Zulus.
Monument Hill, 6km south of Pretoria. Open: daily 9am–4.45pm. Admission charge.

The Randlords

Boers, and to set up a British-ruled Federation of South Africa. This led to the Jameson Raid of 1895, when Dr Leander Starr Jameson, a close friend of Rhodes, led a raiding party into the Transvaal with the aim of bringing about an insurrection. He failed ignominiously.

The most enduring legacy of the Randlords is the economy and society of modern South Africa. Mining affected the lives of everybody. Everything that South Africa subsequently became – and stood for – happened because of mining.

Two of the mighty Randlords. Solly Joel (left) and Cecil Rhodes (below)

The discovery of gold and diamonds in the 19th century not only reversed the fortunes of what had been a remote and poor land making it rich and powerful, but brought vast wealth to a small group of immigrant white men. Cecil John Rhodes, Barney Barnato, Solly Joel, Julius Wernher, Alfred Beit, Max Michaelis and J B Robinson were dubbed the 'Randlords' by the British press. Chief among them was Rhodes, diamond magnate, goldmine owner, politician, empire-builder and founder of Rhodesia.

The Randlords' lives were colourful and controversial. The ultimate plutocrats, they built themselves large mansions in fashionable parts of London, collected art, sponsored foundations and set up scholarships. But wealth brought with it a lust for political power.

Rhodes in particular wanted to topple Paul Kruger, leader of the Transvaal

The last of the Randlords is Harry Oppenheimer, head of De Beers, who provided the resources which kept the flag of liberalism flying, and without whom Helen Suzman could never have fought her solitary battle against apartheid as the only Progressive Federal Party MP during three parliaments. Oppenheimer built bridges to the ANC leadership when to have dealings with them was treasonable, and his efforts greatly assisted de Klerk's overtures to them in later years.

GETTING AWAY FROM IT ALL

'Africa always brings us
something new.'
PLINY THE ELDER
(AD23–79),
Historia Naturalis, Book 8,
Section 42

Train Journeys

South Africa is one of the few remaining countries where you can still experience magical railway journeys in trains of enormous prestige. Make an epic journey conjuring up the romance of a lost age of steam travel, or take a short trip for just a day out or a weekend away.

UNDER STEAM

The Edwardian trains that steamed across Africa signalled the beginning of the end of a still-vivid era of transport riders, tsetse flies and rampaging lions.

THE EPIC JOURNEY
Rovos Rail
The magnificently restored, privately-owned *Pride of Africa*, travels a variety of routes. From Cape Town, destinations include Victoria Falls (Zimbabwe) and Dar es Salaam (Tanzania), with stop-overs at Matjiesfontein, Kimberley and Pretoria, and optional sightseeing *en route*. Twelve coaches are drawn by any of three vintage locomotives used at various stages of the journey. Sleepers, dining car and observation carriages are the refurbished originals, a reminder of pre-war opulence. *PO Box 2837, Pretoria 0001. Tel: 012–323 6052.*

Shongololo Express
Named after a local brown millipede, this new service offers luxurious train rides taking in all the highlights of South Africa from the Kruger National Park to Cape Town.
10 Amelia Street, Dunvegan, Edenvale 1610. Tel: 011–454 1262.

Union Limited
A steam locomotive and original carriages of the old Union Limited, the first luxury train (1923) taking first-class passengers from Johannesburg to Cape Town to meet the ocean liners, have been transformed into a 'safari' train with a variety of routes and destinations. See

The Outeniqua Choo Choo still puffs along between George and Knysna

The Blue Train opposite.
PO Box 4325, Cape Town. Tel: 021–405 4391.

SHORT EXCURSIONS
Banana Express
The Port Shepstone and Alfred Country Railway offers a choice of two trips in KwaZulu/Natal: a 13km round route (2½ hours) from Port Shepstone (see page 103) to Izotsha, which runs through banana and sugar plantations and stops for refreshments at a beachfront hotel; and a six-hour return trip to Paddock, which includes a *braai* (barbecue) at Paddock Station.
PO Box 115, Umtentweni 4235. Tel: 03931–76443. Izotsha: Thursday and Sunday. Paddock: Wednesday and Saturday.

Magaliesberg Express
The South African National Railway and Steam Museum Preservation Group offers day trips from Johannesburg Station to the Magaliesberg (see page 133).
South African National Railway and Steam Museum Preservation Group, PO Box 1419, Roosevelt Park 2129. Tel: 011–888 1154. Twice monthly.

Midmar Steam Railway
This is a narrow-gauge railway at the Midmar Historical Village (see page 99), near Pietermaritzburg. Restored steam engines are in regular weekend use.
Historical Village, Natal Parks Board, Private Bag X6, Howick 3290. Tel: 0332–305930.

Ostrich Express
Operating between Oudtshoorn (see page 60) and Calitzdorp, the train traverses ostrich country and the Karoo.
PO Box 59, Oudtshoorn 6620. Tel:

0443–223540. Weekends only (weekdays, by arrangement).

Outeniqua Choo Choo
This distinguished old steam train covers the George to Knysna section of the Garden Route (see pages 64–5), passing through spectacular scenery.
Outeniqua Choo Choo. Tel: 0441–738202. Weekdays – 4 hours each way.

DIESEL OR ELECTRIC TRAIN TRAVEL

THE BLUE TRAIN
The Blue Train replaced the old Johannesburg–Cape Town Union Limited (see opposite) in 1939. Its name derives from the colour of the old original train. Today's Blue Train is one of the great trains of the world, a slower alternative to flying (Cape Town–Pretoria, 24 hours), but an infinitely superior experience. It has sleeping accommodation ranging from luxury to moderate singles, with shower, a dining and lounge car, and space to carry cars. An additional new Transvaal Lowveld Route, Pretoria to Nelspruit, is an excellent springboard for visits to the Kruger National Park. There are also trips to Victoria Falls in Zimbabwe.
Interpax, PO Box 1111, Johannesburg 2000. Tel: 011–773 7631.

REGULAR PASSENGER SERVICES
Regular intercity trains traverse some amazing landscapes. The best routes are the Trans-Karoo, the Trans-Orange, the Trans-Natal and the Algoa Express. There are a variety of discounts for children and senior citizens.
Interpax, see The Blue Train above for address. Tel: 011–774 4469.

Safaris and Game Reserves

*O*ne of the key attractions of a visit to South Africa is a trip into the bush to experience at first hand nature untamed.

MAKING A SELECTION

Public game reserves, such as the Kruger National Park (see pages 94–5) provide plenty of opportunity for viewing game and are primarily explored in tourists' own vehicles (although game drives are organised at some) and generally involve self-catering ranging from cottages to camp sites. See **Practical Guide**, page 185, for details.

Public nature reserves are not noted for their game so much as for their scenic beauty, and are generally good places for walking, hiking and climbing. See **Practical Guide**, page 186, for details.

Private reserves are not open to the general public. They provide world-class hospitality and accommodation and organise off-the-beaten-track safaris in four-wheel-drive vehicles. See page 174 for details.

WHAT TO TAKE

Wear subdued colours – brown, dark green or khaki: anything bright could alarm the animals. It can be chilly on dawn and dusk drives, so take a jumper and long trousers. Some of the private reserves require 'smart casual' attire for evenings. Binoculars are essential. See **Surviving in the Wilds**, pages 32–3.

WHERE TO SEE THE BIG FIVE

The Big Five – lion, rhino, elephant, buffalo, leopard – can all be seen in the Kruger National Park. This is not the case with every game reserve. Check before making a reservation.

Cape Eco Safaris

Combinations of safaris from Kalahari-dune Tent Safaris to Richtersveld Mountain Desert Safari.

PO Box 7143, North Paarl 7623. Tel: 02211–638334.

The Conservation Corporation
PO Box 1211, Sunninghill Park 2157.
Tel: 011–803 8421 or fax: 011–803 1810.
Lawson's Tours
Photographic and wildlife safaris, hiking
and wilderness trails, and birdwatching
tours. Individuals or small groups.
PO Box 507, Nelspruit 1200. Tel:
01311–552147 or fax: 01311–551793.
Safari Consultants
Orchard House, Upper Road, Little
Cornard, Sudbury, Suffolk CO10 0NZ,
UK. Tel: 01787 228494.

HIKING

Climbers and hikers gravitate to the
Drakensberg and the Cedarberg, two
mountain ranges renowned for their
views and variety of walks and trails.
However, throughout the country,
forests, deserts and coastal habitats are
criss-crossed by hiking trails ranging
from the undemanding to the strenuous.
New trails are being opened up all the
time, and many sections of the National
Hiking Way – a route which will
eventually enable hikers to make a
complete circuit of South Africa on foot
– have been completed.

Some trails provide equipped huts or
tents, while on others you carry your own
lightweight tent. Most require you to
bring your own food. Always remember to
take a water bottle, sun block and a hat,
and be prepared to take advantage of a
dip in a mountain pool. When venturing
into areas far from food and fresh water
supplies, make allowances for emergencies
by taking a survival ration pack including
high-protein biscuits. Check weather
reports before setting off. See also
Surviving in the Wilds, pages 32–3.

Hikers on one of the many trails in the
magnificent Drakensberg Mountains

When the trail is long and hot, a mountain pool
can be very inviting

Places on trails administered by the
National Parks Board and the Natal
Parks Board need to be booked in
advance; most trails, walks and
wilderness areas are open to the public
throughout the year. Some will require
permits. These are neither difficult to
obtain nor expensive.
The Hiking Federation of South
Africa
PO Box 17247, Groenkloof, Pretoria 0027.
Tel: 012–46 7562.
The Mountain Club of South Africa,
97 Hatfield Gardens, Cape Town 8001.
Tel: 021–45 3412.
National Parks Board and the **Natal**
Parks Board, see **Practical Guide**,
page 185.
Information and maps from National
Hiking Way Board, Private Bag X447,
Pretoria 0001. Tel: 012–310 3839.

On the Water

*M*essing about in boats is an obvious choice for those wanting to escape the crowds. Yachting, white-water rafting, canoeing, surfing, windsurfing or just bobbing about in a dinghy are all activities available in abundance.

CANOEING

The season for canoeing varies. In some parts of the country, winter is best because of the rainfall. Elsewhere, summer is preferable. Two punishing canoe marathons, the Hansa Dusi (January) and the KWV Berg River Canoe Marathon (July) attract international paddlers.

Catamaran racing is just one of the many boating possibilities in South Africa

Breede River Adventures
Canoeing and camping on the Breede River (see page 52).
104 Upper Maynard Street, Vredehoek 8001. Tel: 021–461 0033.
The South African Canoe Federation
PO Box 5, McGregor 6708, Western Cape. Tel: 02353–733.

WHITE-WATER RAFTING

This must be one of the most death-defying sports imaginable – and there are infinite possibilities to indulge in it.
River Runners
White-water rafting on the Doring or Orange Rivers.
PO Box 583, Constantia 7848. Tel: 021–762 2350.
Felix Unite, River Adventures
PO Box 96, Kenilworth 7745. Tel: 021–762 6935.

WINDSURFING

See Sport, page 161.

YACHTING

There are a great many possibilities for offshore, dam and ocean sailing and cruising. South Africa has 86 registered yacht clubs, but rental facilities for visitors are limited. Most clubs offer temporary holiday membership to visitors by prior arrangement. The season is all year round. South Africa has a number of major yachting, sailing and cruising events and racing circuits. One of the most magnificent is the Rothmans Week Regatta in the Western Cape which includes three days of round-the-buoys racing, a medium-distance day race and an overnight long-distance race up the West Coast to Saldanha and back.
South African Yacht Racing Association
82 1st Avenue, Dunvegan, Edenvale 1619. Tel: 11–783 4443.
The Cruising Association of South Africa
PO Box 5036, Cape Town 8000. Tel: 021–41 1056.

DIRECTORY

'South Africa is spinning on a hub of gold.'

NEGLEY FARSON,
Behind God's Back, 1940

Shopping

*S*outh Africa has plenty of choice for souvenir-hunters, from recycled coloured glass products to baskets, wire sculpture, springbok *biltong* (see page 164), 1994 election ballot forms, leather goods, shells, port wine and tribal beadwork. Prices vary: high street outlets and shopping malls are the dearest, market stalls less so; roadside vendors are cheapest. South African antiques can be expensive, but a roaring trade in bric-à-brac is worth investigating. Sarongs, T-shirts, sandals, shorts and bathing costumes can all be purchased, and there are plenty of shops featuring the output of local fashion designers.

African 'crafts' are sometimes expensive in shops – particularly when northern-made items are sold in the south. Learn quickly how to be discerning: an object's appearance might be jolly, but quality varies, and prices can escalate depending on how canny the vendor is in summing you up. Haggle in markets (there are weekend fleamarkets in all the major citites), but not in shops.

BEST BUYS
Animal products
This is certainly not a suggestion that you go searching for an elephant-foot umbrella stand – like the one great uncle brought home 70 years ago. Should you be offered one, or indeed anything coming from an elephant (and ivory in particular), report the vendor to the police. However, 'blown' ostrich eggs make unusual souvenirs, and springbok and zebra skins are available from culled animals. Otherwise there are few animal products that any sensitive visitor would want to buy – apart from leather accessories like wallets, bags and belts. Excellent copies do exist, and anyway the real thing looks better on the animal than it does on you.

Basketware
There is a wide range of basketwork, some of the most beautiful made by

A range of fine basketware on offer at Umgababa market near Durban

Wares on sale at the roadside are cheap, but may or may not be worth buying

Sotho and Zulu peoples. Many items – coil-woven baskets, basins, beer-strainers, mats – are still made in the traditional way or have been developed and reinterpreted to make them more commercial and practicable for modern life.

Books and maps
Foreign-published books and magazines are expensive in South Africa. Take holiday reading with you. However, most towns and cities are well covered by book stores and newsagents selling maps and local guides.

Curios, arts and crafts
Local arts and crafts are available in abundance. Sculpted soapstone heads, beaded ashtrays, decorated ostrich eggs, beaten copper panels with elephants in low relief, plastic beaded bracelets and necklaces ... the list is endless. Some of it is lovely, even exquisite. Much of it is cheap tat, the art of Africa bastardised. If you must buy this, then go to one of the 'self-help' organisation's outlets (enquire at local tourist information associations). Such things as enamel mugs with brightly beaded covers and handles are good for picnics, and the beaded spectacle neckchains are very popular, as are carved salad spoons, big wooden dishes, textiles, pottery and beadwork.

Food and wine
Easy to take home is *konfyt* (preserved fruit), sold sealed in jars, dried fruit and *biltong*. Local wines are widely exported though much estate wine is not. Local port and sherry is often cheaper in the manufacturing locale than it is abroad.

See **Food and Drink**, pages 164–5.

Jewellery and gemstones
Cufflinks, necklaces, rings and other items of jewellery are available in a wide range of settings, which include anything from tiger's-eye to diamonds. Gold and diamond jewellery is tax free.

Shells
There are plenty of free shells on the beaches. However, you can also buy them – and they can be very expensive depending on species, condition and origin. Bear in mind that many exotic ones may come from Mauritius. The best places to find shells are Jeffrey's Bay (Eastern Cape), Blouberg Strand (Western Cape) and a good place to buy them is on Durban's seafront stalls. You might also be offered coral. Avoid it; like some of the shells, it has been commercially harvested.

Where to Shop

AFRICAN HERBAL REMEDIES
Johannesburg
KwaDabgulamanzi
Herbal remedies prescribed by a *sangoma* – a witchdoctor and spiritual medium.
16 Diagonal Street, Newtown. Tel: 011–838 7352.

BOOKS AND MAPS
Cape Town
Throughout the city there are branches of **CNA** or **Exclusive Books** (see telephone directory for details).
Clarke's Bookshop
Rare and second-hand books, prints and maps, books on South Africa.
211 Long Street, 8001. Tel: 021–23 5739.

Durban
Branches of **CNA** (see telephone directory for details).
Adams & Co
341 West Street. Tel: 031–304 8571.
Map Centre
Tourist maps of the region.
42 Fisher Street Point. Tel: 031–37 8531.

Johannesburg
Branches of **Exclusive Books** and **CNA** (see telephone directory for details).
Out of Print
Antiquarian books.
3 Market Theatre Shopping Mall. Tel: 011–838 7264.

CURIOS, ARTS AND CRAFTS
Cape Town
African Image
Wire sculpture, music, jewellery, baskets, textiles, signs, pottery and an eclectic mix of ethnic utensils old and new.
52 Burg Street. Tel: 021–23 8385.

Third World Spectator
African pots, baskets, headrests etc.
9 Protea Insurance Building, Green Market Square. Tel: 021–24 2957.

Durban
African Art Centre
Telephone wire *imbenge* (baskets), beaded animals, pottery and so on.
8 Guildhall Arcade, 35 Gardiner Street. Tel: 031–304 7915.

Johannesburg
Kim Sacks Gallery and Craft Centre
Selection of textiles, basketware, jewellery and ceramics.
92a Frances Street, Bellevue. Tel: 011–648 6107.
The Movement Trading Store
The ANC marketing outlet.
Shell House, 51 Plein Street. Tel: 011–330 7000.

JEWELLERY AND GEMSTONES
Cape Town
Penny Murdock Jewellery
Manufacturers and Designers
Top quality bespoke jewellery and a wide range of pieces old and new.
50 Victoria Road, Camps Bay 8001. Tel: 021–438 1600.

Durban
Caney's Jewellers
Well established source of diamond jewellery.
331 West Street. Tel: 031–305 1677.

Johannesburg
Jewel City
Three buildings house 120 gem companies. Movies, talks and advice.

For advice, call the SA Diamond Company, Jewel City, Suite 614, 240 Commissioner Street. Tel: 011–334 2693.

MARKETS
Cape Town
Green Market Square
The city's best. Ethnic clothes, jewellery, curios, junk and books.
Open: Monday to Saturday 8am–5pm.
Green Point Stadium
Electric kettles to second-hand furniture
Open: Sundays and public holidays, weather-permitting, 8am–5pm.
Church Street Antique Market
Sells antiques and junk.
Open: Friday 9am–3pm.

Johannesburg
Newtown Market Africa
Cosmopolitan Saturday hub. Antique African costume, masks, junk, beads.
Newtown Cultural Precinct. Open: Saturday 9am–4pm.

Durban
Grey Street area precinct
Sells saris, saddles, kerosene lamps, incense and sweetmeats.
Victoria Street Market
Best for witchdoctor's potions, carvings, spices, bright patterned fabric, eastern silks, fruit and fish.
Corner of Queen and Russell streets. Tel: 031–306 4021.
Dalton Road Market
This is a Zulu traditional-wear market.
Amphitheatre Market
Fleamarket with over 700 stalls.
North Beach. Open: Sunday.

OUTDOOR EQUIPMENT
Cape Town
Cape Union Mart
Gear for camping, climbing and hiking.

Victoria Wharf, the Waterfront. Tel: 021–419 0019. Branches nationally.
Surf Centre
70 Loop Street, Cape Town 8000. Tel: 021–24 7894.

Durban
Quarter Masters
14 The Workshop, 99 Aliwal Street. Tel: 031–305 3087.
Surf Centre
7 Brickhill Road. Tel: 031–368 3753.

Johannesburg
Outdoor Warehouse
Tents, camping and hiking equipment.
20 Bisset Road, Jet Park. Tel: 011–826 6406.

SHOPPING MALLS
Cape Town
Cavendish Square
High quality shopping, eight cinemas.
Dreyer Street, Claremont. Tel: 021–64 3052. Open: Monday to Saturday 9am–5pm.
Victoria and Alfred Waterfront
Harbourside shops, restaurants and bars.
Victoria and Alfred Waterfront. Tel: 021–418 2350.

Durban
The Wheel
Over 100 speciality shops, restaurants and bars. Twelve cinemas.
Gillespie Street. Tel: 031–32 4324.

Johannesburg
Sandton City
The last word in shopping mall culture – you can buy virtually anything here.
Between Rivonia Road, 5th Street and Sandton Drive. Tel: 011–783 7413.
Carlton Centre
See page 115.

Entertainment

*C*onnoisseurs increasingly acknowledge the rich diversity of South African culture, the result of contact between African traditions and a variety of immigrant cultures. In addition, artists of world fame, who have started visiting the country again since the gradual lifting of the cultural embargo, along with returning exiled artists, are all influencing the home-grown arts.

BALLET AND DANCE

Dance has always been an integral part of African life: it is an element in the hunt, waging war, courting, marriage, initiation and work. Non-African dance traditions have also blossomed despite the cultural boycott. There are three ballet companies – Pact Ballet, Capab Ballet, and the Napac Dance Company – as well as independent groups and ensembles in Cape Town, Durban and Johannesburg, some of which train black dancers with no previous experience.

The development of the South African dance tradition over the last two decades cannot be divorced from performance and protest theatre, with its mixture of song, movement and dance. The protest musical has established certain styles of dancing and stage techniques: the *toyi-toyi* (struggle dance of the people); the *mapantsula* (township jive); *isicatamiya* (a choir tradition from the mines and men's hostels); and traditional Zulu dances.

THEATRE

South Africa's two established theatrical traditions – the native African and introduced European – have been joined by a third, hybrid theatre which has developed over recent decades. While it contains elements of both the original forms, it is anchored in the performance form of the African tradition, displaying its characteristics with interesting popular urban variations. It has ritual and symbolism; it involves the spectators; it has a strong musical base and narrative elements; and dance is integral to it. In addition to this, cabaret, dance-drama, one-person shows, narratives, children's theatre, musicals and satire are all of significance in the developing theatre tradition.

Cape Town
The Baxter
Main Road, Rondebosch. Tel: 021–685 7880.
Dock Road Theatre
Victoria and Alfred Waterfront. Tel: 021–419 7722.
Maynardville Open Air Theatre
Wynberg. For tickets, call Computicket, tel: 021–21 4715.
Nico Malan Theatre
DF Malan Street. Tel: 021–21 5470.
Theatre on the Bay
Link Street, Camps Bay. Tel: 021–438 3300.

Durban
The Natal Playhouse
Four separate theatres: The Cellar, The Drama, The Loft and The Studio.
Smith Street. Tel: 031–304 3631.

Johannesburg
Alhambra Theatre
109 Sivewright Avenue, Doornfontein. Tel: 011–402 6174.

A traditional Zulu dance performed at the Zulu village in Assegay Safari Park near Durban

Civic Theatre
Loveday Street Extension, Braamfontein.
Tel: 011–304 3408.
Market Theatre Laboratory
Market Precinct. Tel: 011–836 6499.
Market Theatre
Wolhuter Street, Newtown. Tel: 011–832 1641.
Rex Garner Theatre
109 Sivewright Avenue, Doornfontein.
Tel: 011–402 6174.
Windybrow Theatre
Windybrow Centre for the Arts, 161 Nugget Street, Hillbrow. Tel: 011–720 7094.

CINEMA

The South African film industry is developing slowly. In recent years films based on texts by Afrikaans writers have been produced, but only latterly has the industry begun to reflect the country's cultural diversity. Certain local and national film festivals (see pages 150–1) ensure the circulation of ideas, and Cape Town in particular is developing a promising film culture.

Ster-Kinekor and Nu Metro, the two largest distributors of films in South Africa, have screens all over the country.

Drive-in cinemas can still be found. A few of the more interesting cinemas are listed below:
Cape Town
Baxter
Main Road, Rondebosch. Tel: 021–685 7880.
Imax
Victoria and Alfred Waterfront.
Tel: 021–21 4715.
The Labia
Orange Street, Gardens. Tel: 021–24 5927.
The **South African National Gallery** frequently shows documentaries and films by local independent filmmakers. Check their listings sheets.

Durban
Museum Theatre
Free lunch-hour films run by the Reference Library.
1st Floor, City Hall.

Johannesburg
Seven Arts Cinema
Grant Avenue, Norwood. Tel: 011–473 1680.
Art Circuit Cinema
Rosebank Mall. Tel: 011–880 2866.

Music

Although there is a still a clear polarisation between European music and African-based ethnic music, a shift in emphasis indicates a fusion of the two styles. Opera and particularly choir music are the two areas where all population groups mix. Private sponsorship nurtures 'serious' classical music, while its composers are increasingly inspired by the country's ethnic diversity. Popular music is beginning to take on an African character, and black musicians are regarded as key figures of pop music, jazz and Afro-rock. Township jazz and blues, and especially the development of *kwela* music in the 1940s and 1950s were hampered by apartheid. Black and Coloured musicians are now reinventing and refining the music of those days. To see the results, go to the nightclubs. Most sell drink, some have food.

CLASSICAL MUSIC AND OPERA
Cape Town
Cape Town City Hall
Cape Town Symphony Orchestra. Weekly concerts (Tuesday and Sunday). *Darling Street. Tel: 021–461 7084.*
Nico Malan Opera House
Cape Town Symphony Orchestra. *DF Malan Street, Foreshore. Tel: 021–217 695*

Durban
The Opera, Natal Playhouse
Seat of the Natal Philharmonic Orchestra. Weekly concerts. *Smith Street. Tel: 031–304 3631.*

Johannesburg
City Hall
National Symphony Orchestra performances. *President Street, Johannesburg. Tel: 011–331 9991.*

CLUBS
In each city, many venues come and go with the season. Check the local listings.
Cape Town
Bree Street Shebeen
Best township music. *Bree Street. Tel: 021–419 4941.*
Club Ubuntu
Township-style jazz. *NY1 Shopping Centre, Guguletu. Tel: 021–419 4732.*

Durban's opera house and theatre is also home to the Natal Philharmonic Orchestra

Dock Road Café
Various theme bars including jazz, funk and disco.
Victoria and Alfred Waterfront.
Tel: 021–419 7722.
The Music Workshop
Corner of Station Road and Drake Street, Observatory. Tel: 021–488 2516.

Durban
Africafé
Brightly coloured ethnic venue.
Smith Street Arcade. Tel: 031–301 0890.
Baghdad Café
American theme bar with stage for concerts.
72 Winder Street.
Behind the Moon
Cool jazz club.
550 Point Road. Tel: 031–32 6892.
Three Thirty
Seething, popular dancefloor.
330 Point Road, Durban.

Johannesburg
The Bass Line
Jazz.
7th Street, Mellville. Tel: 011–482 6915.
Kippies in the Market
A mix of jazz, Afro-jazz, jazz fusion and blues.
Wolhuter Street, Newtown Cultural Precinct. Tel: 011–643 4212.

Kwela Shebeen
Kwela, jazz and African soul.
Rivonia Mews, Rivonia Boulevard, Rivonia.
Tel: 011–803 5435.
Get Ahead Shebeen
Too scared to visit the real thing in Soweto? Then come here. Live music by big names like Mahlatini and the Mahotella Queens. Good food and bar,
Oxford Road, Rosebank. Tel: 011–442 5964.
Mojo's
Jazz, and good food.
206 Louis Botha Avenue, Orange Grove.
Tel: 011–483 1282.

OPEN-AIR VENUES
Cape Town
Oude Libertas Amphitheatre
Classical music and dance.
Stellenbosch. Tel: 021–808 7473.
Kirstenbosch Summer Sunset Concerts
Jazz, steelbands, classical music, choirs.
Kirstenbosch National Botanical Gardens, Rhodes Drive, Newlands. Tel: 021–762 1166.

Calendar of Events

JANUARY–DECEMBER
Waterfront Arts and Crafts Market
Over 160 stalls in the country's largest indoor crafts market at the Victoria and Alfred Waterfront, Cape Town.

JANUARY
Cape Coon Carnival
More than 12,000 minstrels in colourful costumes sing and dance their way through the streets of Cape Town.

FEBRUARY
Johannesburg Biennale
A major contemporary art event (exhibitions and installations) will bring international visual artists to work and exhibit with local artists.

FEBRUARY–MARCH
Cape Show
The Cape's biggest annual show features equestrian events, sheep shearing and live entertainment. There is also a funfair, farmyard and miniature train. (Cape Town.)

MARCH
Central (Rainbow) Show
Lasting ten days, this is supposedly the biggest saddle-horse show of its kind in the southern hemisphere. Special events, sports, fireworks and live entertainment. (Bloemfontein.)

APRIL
Rand Easter Show
Africa's biggest and most popular consumer show. (Johannesburg.)
Paarl Nouveau Wine Festival
In celebration of harvest's end, and as part of this event, the first wines of the

season are carried up the slopes of Paarl Mountain in a variety of novel ways from hot-air balloons to donkeys. Wine tasting, refreshments and music. (Paarl, Western Cape.)
Johannesburg Pop Festival
Alfresco musical entertainment with contemporary popular music performed by some of South Africa's finest artists.
Natal Mercury Durban Designer Collection (DDC)
KwaZulu/Natal's premier fashion show culminates in a gala show at which a winning designer is announced.

MAY
Face to Face Youth Arts Festival
A 10-day programme of music, drama and fine arts held at various venues. (Durban.)
Royal Show
Competitive classes for livestock, agricultural products, crafts and home industries provide the backbone of this show. (Pietermaritzburg.)

JUNE/JULY
Standard Bank National Arts Festival
South Africa's premier annual cultural event reflects the diversity of a dynamic artistic community. Opera, choral music, bands, jazz and recitals plus Fringe, arts and crafts and film. (Grahamstown.)

JULY
The Durban Tattoo
With its brass bands, music and military parades, this event is in the same league as the Edinburgh Military Tattoo and London's Royal Tournament.
Durban International Film Festival
Screenings of films from all over the

There's a wide variety of sparkling events all over the country throughout the year

world including Russia, China and Turkey.

SEPTEMBER
Weekly Mail Film Festival
International Film Festival which features independent cinema from around the world. It also promotes independent South African and African cinema. (Johannesburg, Durban and Cape Town.)
Wildlife Exhibition
Designed to enhance appreciation of the environment. There are live exhibits (game and marine life), exhibitions on ecotourism, adventure options, safari, etc (Durban.)

SEPTEMBER–OCTOBER
International Eisteddfod of South Africa
International musicians, folkdancers, brass bands, soloists, massed choirs and orchestras compete in this prestigious event. (Roodepoort, Gauteng.)

Guinness Johannesburg Jazz Festival
South African jazz musicians are among the world's best. Here, at the Market Theatre Complex, they play alongside top international stars.

OCTOBER
Nedbank Proms
One of the highlights of the country's music calendar. Orchestral, choral and chamber music feature the Cape Town Symphony Orchestra, the Cape Town Symphonic Choir and the Cape Welsh Choir. (Cape Town.)
Stellenbosch Food and Wine Festival
Wine estates and wholesalers from the Stellenbosch area display vintages while patrons sample and buy wine and regional cuisine.
The Getaway Outdoor Adventure Show
Outdoor enthusiasts will find a range of leisure activities highlighted here, from scuba diving to camel safaris and hot-air ballooning. (Johannesburg.)

Children

South Africans are generally well disposed towards children, both their own and other people's, and South Africa is a great country to grow up in. With the emphasis on alfresco living, children – even on a short visit – can enjoy plenty of outdoor pursuits. The 'kids' culture' is very American: youngsters follow US trends, fashions, pop stars, films, television and, as almost everywhere, prefer American-style food.

For visiting children, South Africa is a safe country, though you should be extra vigilant on the beach and in the sea (see below). The story is, sadly, not quite the same for the locals, particularly those living in the townships and especially those who have been the victims of apartheid. 'Street children' – orphans and runaways – are everywhere, begging and living on the pavement.

Tour train at Gold Reef City, Johannesburg

TRAVELLING WITH CHILDREN

All the essentials, from nappies to sterilisers via books, tapes and games, are readily available. Bear in mind that distances between locations can be very long, so take games and books to relieve the boredom on drives. It is often a good idea to leave very early, before sunrise, so that you travel before it gets hot and while the children are still sleepy. Make frequent stops. You will find motorway service stations are mushrooming, together with a wide range of facilities, including lavatories, fast food, shops and overnight accommodation. Restaurants tend to have an excellent attitude towards children, usually offering a children's menu or half portions. There is an abundance of child-specific restaurants such as the cheap and cheerful Steer and Spur chains.

ON THE BEACH

Before you head for the beach with children, make sure you observe certain golden rules. The African seas are beguiling; they're also treacherous. Dangerous currents, riptides and backwash can be dangerous – for adults too. Never take these seas for granted, and never let children go swimming unattended or allow them out into the surf on lilos. If the beach is packed but nobody is swimming, then there is probably a good reason for it. Many

Roller-coaster waterslides provide a thrill at Durban's Waterworld

beaches do have lifeguards though they are not on duty around the clock. Around the Cape Peninsula, up the coast and particularly in KwaZulu/Natal, many beaches have safe tidal pools which are ideal for children.

If you plan to spend the day on the beach take not only sunblock (see **Health**, page 184), but bicarbonate of soda which, when mixed into a paste with water, is very effective against bluebottle stings. Don't forget to take drinking water, a sun umbrella, hats, nets and other equipment for the abundant rock pools littering the coast.

HAVING FUN

Most towns and cities have some form of activity to keep children happy – seaside pursuits in some, the zoo in Pretoria, elsewhere just letting off steam in the many open spaces. The air is clean on the whole – though asthma sufferers visiting cities (Johannesburg in particular) should come prepared. All the National Parks are well equipped to cater for the needs of children, with playgrounds, swimming pools and a variety of natural attractions. Trails are graded according to the ability of the walker, and accommodation is generally childproof. Note that some private reserves have age restrictions.

IN TOUCH WITH NATURE

South Africa is paradise for children who want to run wild outdoors, and it's heaven for parents who want a few days of peace and quiet. Pack them off, for a fee, to a weekend or a week in the wilds where, under supervision, they can explore, birdwatch, hike, sail, swim, learn bushcraft or find out about ecology and conservation. However, before you dispatch your offspring, make sure they're fit, and check the level of supervision at the destination. See **Tour Operators**, page 188, for addresses.

CONTEMPORARY ART IN THE NEW SOUTH AFRICA

South Africa's art is only now taking its place in the global cultural arena after its long exclusion, and the international art world, in its constant hunt for a new angle on the human condition, suspects that this newcomer might provide some fresh insights. The country is often regarded as a microcosm of the world: it embodies all the global issues of white and black, rich and poor, developed and underdeveloped.

Until now South African art has had a peculiarly hybrid identity, the

Right: Sotho-style abrstract painting
Below: open-air exhibition in Cape Town

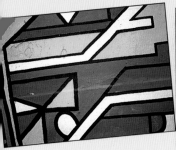

Black African painters are adept in both traditional and European idioms

result of two quite distinct traditions, on the one hand European and harking back to colonialism, and on the other reflecting an African spiritual background. Both were affected by mutual contact and by the realities of recent history. The Western tradition strove to find ways of accommodating itself to the reality of Africa, while colonialism and apartheid shaped and transformed elements of African tradition.

Today South African art is acquiring a new and unique identity. The cultural boycott, instigated by the ANC in exile and enforced by the United Nations, severed the umbilical cord linking the country with America and Europe, and black and white artists began to develop a sense of their own South Africanness. Many black artists, long working in isolation, already felt this. But the boycott also profoundly affected the work of several white artists who no longer felt constrained by mainstream international art movements.

South Africa is beginning to rid itself of the 'baggage' of an historically divided society. Once there was 'township art' and 'protest art'. Then, with the political upheaval and change, came 'transitional art'. Now there is 'South African art' and – for black artists at least – the old formulas of silent suffering are no longer appropriate. Some artists are already redefining art so that it makes sense for South Africa's new society.

Sport

*T*o South Africans sport is almost a religion. In the sunny outdoors, the appeal is the same, whether an event is a spectator game, an impromptu match in a township backyard or a hefty mountain hike.

The options for participating in or watching competitive sport are enormous, while non-competitive outdoor activity like tennis or sailing involves much socialising. A 3,200km-long coastline creates favourable conditions for all ocean sports. The Drakensberg mountains, extending from the Eastern Cape through KwaZulu/

Hot-air ballooning provides an exciting way of seeing the varied landscape

Natal, the Free State and into the Eastern Transvaal, provide an ideal setting for hiking, mountaineering and aerosports like ballooning and hang-gliding. The rivers of the escarpment provide ideal conditions for canoeing and trout fishing.

Spectators are well catered for. Athletics, cricket, rugby, soccer and golf fixtures always attract capacity crowds, and there are prime venues in Cape

Town, Durban and Johannesburg. In the contemporary international arena, South Africa is still something of an unknown quantity as a result of its boycott during the apartheid era. The effect of this was apparent at the 1994 Commonwealth Games in Canada, when South Africa could manage only a meagre 11 medals. The last time South Africa competed in those Games, in 1958, its athletes brought home 31 medals including 13 golds and 10 silvers. Cape Town is a strong contender for the 2004 Olympic Games which gives a glimmer of hope for the future, as does the Confederation of African Football's decision that South Africa will stage the 1996 African Nations Cup.

AERIAL SPORTS

Gliding, hang-gliding, hot-air ballooning and power flying are all possible in South Africa. Table Mountain and the Seven Sisters are favourite hang-gliding sites, and there are many others in the Drakensberg, each graded according to the licences required for them. The country's largest hot-air ballooning club is in Johannesburg with affiliates in Cape Town and Durban. There are rental facilities (with a valid pilot licence) and passenger rides are offered. The Annual Experimental Aircraft Association Margate Air Show happens in May in KwaZulu/Natal. With parachute jumping, flying displays and early aircraft relics, it is the southern hemisphere's largest air show.

South Africa back on the international cricket scene: batting against Australia in 1994

The Aero Club of South Africa
PO Box 9, Johannesburg 2000.
Tel: 011–783 8840.
Balloon Safaris
PO Box 67, Randburg 2125.
Tel: 011–705 3201.

CRICKET

Cricket is a major event on the South African spectator sport calendar. International cricket is played at Newlands Pavilion in Cape Town, at the St George's Park Cricket Oval in Port Elizabeth (South Africa's oldest cricket ground) and the attractive Wanderers ground in Johannesburg.
South African Cricket Union
PO Box 55009, Northlands 2116, Johannesburg 1620. Tel: 011–880 2810.

CYCLING

This is one of the country's favourite outdoor activities. Relatively few people cycle to work but, at weekends and on public holidays, bikes are out in force, the cyclists driven by the keep-fit bug or the need simply to relax on a scenic road. The annual 105km Argus Cycle Tour around the Cape Peninsula attracts 21,000 riders and is a major annual sporting fixture.
The South African Cycling Federation
The professional cycling body.
PO Box 28, Bloemfontein 9300.
Tel: 051–74685.
The Pedal Power Association of Southern Africa
Handles enquiries on recreational cycling.
PO Box 6503, Roggebaai 8012.
Tel: 021–96 4044.
Both the above bodies will assist groups or individuals with planning, advice and the hire of bicycles.

> '...sport has been an icebreaker in bringing reconciliation. I believe sport will play a positive, constructive role in the nation-building process.'
> F W DE KLERK, State President, 1993

EQUESTRIAN SPORTS

The opportunities for riding in South Africa are almost limitless, with no shortage of private riding stables. People ride on beaches, on country trails and in game parks, and pony trekking on weekend or week trips – particularly in Lesotho – is very popular. Polo takes place mostly in KwaZulu/Natal, and there are important racing, dressage and show jumping fixtures in the Western Cape, Gauteng and KwaZulu/Natal. The Metropolitan Stakes, in Cape Town in January, the Administrators Cup, held at Gosforth Park in Johannesburg in March, and the Rothmans July Handicap held at Greyville in Durban in July, are the premier racing fixtures. The October Dunhill Show Jumping Derby and November's Mercedes Riders Show Jumping Championships both take place in Johannesburg.

The South African National Equestrian Federation
PO Box 69414, Bryanston, 2021. Tel: 011–701 3062.
The South African Polo Association
PO Box 42, Pietermaritzburg 3200. Tel: 0331–429909.
The Jockey Club of South Africa
PO Box 74439, Turfontein 2140. Tel: 011–683 9283.
The South African National Pony Club
For enquiries about pony trekking.
9 Roxburghe Avenue, Craighall Park 2196. Tel: 011–887 1800.

FOOTBALL

Football or soccer is very popular among black South Africans, and it has been a conspicuously multiracial sport for years. The Soweto teams Kaizer Chiefs and Orlando Pirates are the draw cards of South Africa's football scene.

Johannesburg boasts a new stadium, Soccer City, that holds 130,000 spectators.
National Football Association
PO Box 910, Johannesburg 2000. Tel 011–474 3522.

GOLF

Golf is immensely popular. Clubs and courses are found in urban centres and mountain, coastal and inland resorts. Some of the best are in and around Cape Town, Durban, Johannesburg, Pretoria and Plettenberg Bay, while the coast south of Durban (the so-called 'Golf Coast'), the Garden Route and the Eastern Transvaal are littered with fine courses. Golf kit is available for hire at hotels with their own courses. Costs for rounds vary, and in most cases are inclusive of green fees, caddy fees and tips. Visitors are welcome at most clubs during the week by prior arrangement. The Lexington PGA Golf Tournament, which takes place every summer, is an impressive line-up of the country's best players, while December's Million Dollar Golf Challenge at Sun City provides an opportunity to watch world-class players battling for golf's biggest cash prize.
The South African Golf Union
Member of the World Amateur Golf Council.
PO Box 1537, Cape Town 8000. Tel: 021–461 7585.
Golf Coast Tours
Natal South Coast Publicity, PO Box 1253, Margate 4275. Tel: 03931–22322.

HIKING AND MOUNTAINEERING
See page 139.

HUNTING

South Africa is internationally regarded as the hunter's mecca. It is the only place in the world where the Big Five may be hunted legally. Hunting is strictly regulated, and is commonly regarded as an acceptable use of a large and growing natural resource.

Professional Hunters' Association of South Africa
PO Box 770, Cramerview 2060, Johannesburg. Tel: 011–706 7724.

RUGBY

Rugby is perhaps the sport for which South Africa is best known. Its national team has been a formidable opponent in international matches. The rugby team is collectively known as the 'Springboks', but this title can in fact refer to any sports team which has represented South Africa and received its national sporting colours. The 1995 Rugby World Cup, which South Africa won, was the biggest sports event ever to be held in the country.

South African Rugby Board
PO Box 99 Newlands 7725. Tel: 021–685 3038.

TENNIS

This is an all-year-round sport; courts feature prominently at hotels, resorts, clubs and private homes throughout the country. Many clubs welcome visitors, and some (like hotels) hire out equipment.

South African Tennis Union
PO Box 2211, Johannesburg 2000. Tel: 011–402 3580.

The Springboks (in green) battle it out against New Zealand on the rugby field

Rod and line at sunset, St Lucia

WATER SPORTS

CANOEING
See page 140.

FISHING
Deep-sea and game fishing
The areas for deep-sea and game fishing are the South Coast, Durban, Sodwana Bay, Richard's Bay and St Lucia (all in KwaZulu/Natal), and Hout Bay, Simon's Town and Hermanus (Western Cape). Best times are, in the north, December to June, in the south, mid-October to November and March to mid-May. The deep-sea fishing season is November to April (for marlin and sail fish) in the north, and September to April (long-fin and yellow-fin tunny) in the south. Boats are available for charter; prices include equipment, bait and rods.
South African Game Fishing Association
PO Box 723, Bedfordview 2008. Tel: 011–53 1847.
The South African Ski-boat, Light Tackle Game Fishing Association
PO Box 4191, Cape Town 8000. Tel: 021–21 3611.
Bluefin Charters
PO Box 44, Kommetjie 7976. Tel: 021–783 1756.

Freshwater fishing
There is public and private freshwater fishing in rivers and dams. Access to private areas is by prior arrangement with the owner or local club; permission is not needed to fish in public waters, though some areas require a licence. The main areas for trout fishing are KwaZulu/Natal, Transvaal and the Western Cape (licences compulsory in proclaimed trout angling waters).
South African Anglers Union
For general enquiries.
26 Douglas Street, Horizon View, Roodepoort 1725. Tel: 011–726 5000.
South African Freshwater Angling Association
PO Box 700, Vereeniging 1930. Tel: 016–22 1552.
South African Rock and Surf Angling Association
28 Silverleaf Avenue, Wynberg, 7800. Tel: 021–219 2629.
Apply for trout fishing permits to:
Transvaal Nature Conservation Division
Private Bag X209, Pretoria 0001. Tel: 012–201 2361;
Natal Parks, Game and Fish Preservation Board
PO Box 662, Pietermaritzburg 3200. Tel: 0331-5 1221; or
Department of Nature and Environmental Conservation
PO Box 9086, Cape Town 8000. Tel: 021–45 0227.

SURFING
South Africa has some of the best surfing in the world, and the South African leg of the international surfing circuit, the Gunston 500 International Surfing Championship, is the country's premier

event. There are eight major surfing areas: Cape Town, the Garden Route, Port Elizabeth, East London, KwaZulu/Natal's north and south coasts, Durban and Richard's Bay. Winter is the best time.

South African Surfing Association
PO Box 617, Umtentweni 4235. Tel: 0391–21150.

UNDERWATER SPORTS
Skin and scuba diving are popular, particularly around the Cape Peninsula, False Bay and the East Coast (Port Elizabeth and Plettenberg Bay) where old wrecks and rich fauna abound; the best time is March. Spearfishing is good off the south coast, where the warm Agulhas meets the cold Benguela current.

South African Underwater Union
PO Box 201, Rondebosch 7700. Tel: 021–69 8531.

WATERSKIING
There is waterskiing on inland lakes and dams as well as off shore. Equipment is available for rent by prior arrangement from local clubs. The best months are October to April.

South African Waterski Association
PO Box 68834, Bryanston 2021. Tel: 011–440 6421.

WHITE-WATER RAFTING
See page 140.

WINDSURFING
There is all-year-round windsurfing on inland lakes and seaside lagoons (off-shore windsurfing is problematical). The Windsurfer Class National Championships, South Africa's No 1 amateur event, occurs in Port Elizabeth in July.

South African Windsurfing Class Association
For equipment hire.
Private Bag X16, Auckland Park 2006. Tel: 011–726 7076.

Windsurfing Africa
33 Stanley Avenue, Milner Park Johannesburg 2000. Tel: 011–726 7076.

YACHTING
See page 140.

Windsurfing is just one of the many first-class water sports on offer in South Africa

Food and Drink

*O*nly a few dishes, predominantly black African ones, are truly indigenous to South Africa. The country's culinary tradition derives from the cuisines of a variety of nations. Imported recipes, subtly adapted over the centuries with the inclusion of local ingredients and the introduction of innovative cooking methods, have given it its originality.

Game on the menu at Gold Reef City

OUTSIDE INFLUENCES

When the Dutch arrived in the 17th century, they found a long-established nomadic way of life, with the Khoikhoi hunting sprinkbok and the San hunting game and gathering veld food. As farms were established new types of food appeared on the southern African scene. The first Dutch settlers introduced the custom of serving vegetables like pumpkin and squash with butter and a sprinkling of grated ginger. One of the chief contributions of the French Huguenots, apart from their improvements to viticulture and the production of fruit, lies in their method of making *confitures* from the local fruit – it survives in the present-day preserves called *konfyt*. Likewise, from German settlers is derived a love of spicy *wurst*, found nowadays in the wide variety of *boerewors* recipes, and hearty casseroles. British settlers introduced roast meats; roast beef and Yorkshire pudding is still the preferred Sunday lunch in many homes – even better if followed by steamed or baked pudding.

Perhaps the greatest contribution of all came from Malay political exiles and slaves brought to the Cape in the 17th century and in great demand as cooks in Dutch homes. It was they who first gave South Africans their taste for sweet and sour combinations, spicy sauces, curries, chutneys and pickles. Immigrant workers from Bengal brought rice, coloured and flavoured with *borrie* (turmeric), and Indian food – South African-style – has taken on board local influences from Malay (raisins and bananas), English colonial and spicy southeast Asian cooking.

BLACK AFRICAN CUISINE

In rural South Africa, traditional food practices are still adhered to where possible, while in the poor townships, lacking clean water and with bustling markets and shanty restaurants, there is a distinct taste for meats and sausages cooked on the open fire.

Traditional southern African food is very healthy: unrefined cereals, dried legumes, vegetables and fruits, animal protein from chicken and milk, red meat from goats and cattle (consumed infrequently), some protein from mopani worms, grasshoppers, ants and edible beetles, low intake of animal fat, salt and sugar and very low consumption of tea and coffee. Traditional drinks are based on fresh water and sour milk. The cooking methods (steaming, stir frying with very little fat or oil and barbecuing over an open fire) and diet are virtually what doctors in the West are recommending today.

Of the traditional foods still being served in African homes, sorghum, maize, and beans are the most popular. Sorghum (the botanical name for a family of grass-like plants) is Africa's only native cereal. Various dishes are made from it, but its use in beer-making is considered the most important. For the modern table, a mixture of sorghum, tomato, peppers and onions, and French salad dressing is an interesting contribution to South African cuisine.

The Portuguese navigators first brought maize to western Africa; of the various dishes made from it, porridge is the most popular. Wild spinach is a favourite, and there are many other dishes made from such ingredients as pumpkin, sweet potato, wild melons, fruit – and insects (11 species are well known in South African cooking, including fried ants or grasshoppers). Most of these have never been eaten by the majority of South Africans.

Fast food in a rural setting

FOODS TO LOOK OUT FOR

Biltong

Biltong, a savoury dried meat, came to the Cape with Dutch settlers whose *tassal*, a simpler version, was adapted to the less pungent *biltong*. The best *biltong* is made from the meat of kudu, springbok, warthog or ostrich, or from beef.

Bobotie

Ground lamb flavoured with turmeric and other eastern spices, covered with an egg custard and baked slowly in the oven. Served with yellow rice and raisins, and stewed fruits such as apricots, peaches and prunes.

THE BRAAI

Braaivleis (grilled meat) cooked on the *braai* (barbecue) is more a way of life than a culinary experience – especially among whites – as witness the old radio jingle advertising a certain car: '*Braaivleis*, rugby, sunny skies and Chevrolet.' *Boerewors*, chops, steak, or *sosaties*, and occasionally fish, are grilled over an open flame outdoors, then eaten with salad and washed down with beer and wine. The *braai*, accompanied by much licking of fingers, epitomises a laid-back, relaxed lifestyle. Generally a summertime event, it is a social ritual with its own peculiar etiquette.

Roadside vendor of *biltong*, the dried meat that sustained the early Dutch settlers

slowly, preferably in a cast-iron pot over the coals. Almost any vegetable can be used – though tomato, pumpkin, green bean, *veldkool* (wild asparagus) or *waterblommetjie* (water lily flowers) are the most popular.

Boerewors

Traditionally, a self-sufficient farming community wastes nothing. When a beast was slaughtered in winter, all parts were used, including the intestines, which were used as casings for homemade sausages filled with anything from beef and mutton to game meat or even game offal. No *braai* (see opposite) is complete without *boerewors*.

Bredies

Bredies are stews made from lamb or mutton and vegetables, cooked very

Bunny-chow

A Durban phenomenon: a quarter loaf of bread is hollowed out and filled with bean curry. The inside is replaced as a lid.

Cape brandy pudding

Wonderfully moist baked pudding with dates and nuts and flavoured with Cape brandy. Served with fresh cream.

Frikkadels

Extremely popular in Holland in the 17th and 18th centuries, these meatballs were introduced by the Dutch settlers.

Green mealie on the cob
An end-of-summer snack, roasted over
an open brazier. Crispy and chewy.

Karoo lamb and mutton
Today the best mutton and lamb come
from the Karoo or the grasslands of
Natal and the Free State. Many old
recipes require fat mutton – see *bredies* –
though modern tastes differ wildly.

A buffet with sliced *biltong*, *boerewors* spirals
and chicken *sosaties* (above); with *bobotie* (left)

pickled fish (firm white fish) was
perfected by the Malays. If you don't get
the chance to taste the home-made
version, buy it at the Woolworths
supermarket.

Potjiekos
Game was often cooked in a black cast-
iron *potjie* (pot) on three legs over the fire
for hours until tender. Springbok is the
preferred meat.

Prawns *peri-peri*
A dish brought to South Africa by
Portuguese settlers from Mozambique
and Angola. Prawns are marinated in
olive oil, lemon juice, garlic, bay leaves,
peri-peri powder (made from chillies) and
ground cloves before cooking.

Pumpkin fritters
A great South African favourite, these are
served either as a vegetable or a pudding.

Sosaties
Skewered lamb (kebab-style) marinated
in a curry sauce that originated in Java.

Koeksisters
These tamer cousins of Malay
sweetmeats consist of nut or fruit
doughs, either boiled or fried in fat then
preserved in honey or a thick syrup of
concentrated fruit juices.

Oysters on the shell
Oysters occur naturally along the south
and east coasts of the Cape. Cultivated
oysters from Knysna are especially good.

Pickled fish
One of the best-known Cape dishes,

Where to Eat and Drink

Many restaurants do not have a liquor licence which means you bring your own drinks. Others only have a wine and malt licence, restricting diners to wine and beer. Check before you go.

Price Guide
R up to R40
RR between R40 and R65
RRR over R65

WESTERN CAPE AND EASTERN CAPE

CAPE TOWN AND ENVIRONS
Africa Café R
Wide variety of pan-African choices.
213 Lower Main Road, Observatory, Cape Town. Tel: 021–47 9553. Open for dinner Monday to Saturday. Booking advisable.
Arlindo's RR
Seafood and game are featured strongly.
Shop 155, Victoria Wharf, Victoria and Alfred Waterfront. Tel: 021–21 6888. Lunch or dinner, booking advisable.
The Brass Bell R
Busy upstairs restaurant and lower-level pub overlooking Kalk Bay harbour. Predominantly seafood.
Kalk Bay Railway Station. Tel: 021–788 5455. Dinner is best. Booking advisable.
Constantia Uitsig RRR
French and Italian country food.
Uitsig Farm, Constantia. Tel: 021–794 4480.
Fish on the Rocks R
Fish (or calamari) and chips take-away.
Harbour Road, Hout Bay. Tel: 021–790 1152. Open: daily. There are other similar venues here, on the portside.
Fisherman's Cottage RR
Continental food in historic cottage.

3 Gray Road, Plumstead. Tel: 021–797 6341. Lunch Tuesday to Friday, dinner Tuesday to Saturday. Booking essential.
Floris Smit Huijs RR
Eclectic array of dishes culled from the world over. Pleasant central venue.
55 Church Street, Cape Town. Tel: 021–23 3414. Lunch Monday to Friday, dinner Monday to Saturday. Booking essential.

For a drink
Alphen Hotel
Alphen Drive, Constantia. Tel: 021–794 5011.
The Crow Bar
43 Waterkant Street, Cape Town. Tel: 021–419 3660.
Ferryman's Tavern
East Pier Road, Waterfront, Cape Town. Tel: 021–419 7748.

Cape Town Coffee Shops
Natale Labia Coffee Shop
192 Main Road, Muizenberg. Tel: 021–788 4106.
The Quarterman Deck
Jubilee Square, Simon's Town. Tel: 021–786 3825.
Rhodes Memorial Tea Garden
Groote Schuur Estate, Rondebosch. Tel: 021–689 9151.
Zerbans Cake and Coffee Shop
Gardens Centre. Tel: 021–461 1594.

FRANSCHHOEK
La Petite Ferme RR
Unfussy, delicious farm-fresh food.
Franschhoek Pass Road, Franschhoek. Tel: 02212–3016. Open: daily for lunch and tea. Booking essential.
Le Quartier Français RR
An extensive and varied menu has, for

English nostalgia at Howick

example, curried snoek with creamed sweet potato and spiced tomato-onion *smoor*, or braised leg of lamb steaks.
Main Road. Tel: 02212–2151. Lunch daily, dinner Monday to Saturday. Magnificent setting for alfresco dining. Booking advisable.

GARDEN ROUTE
Hunter's Country House RRR
An elegant country getaway famous for outstanding, hearty food.
National Road, between Knysna and Plettenberg Bay. Tel: 04457–7818.
Knysna Protea Hotel RR
Have a pub lunch by the pool, perhaps including the famous Knysna oysters.
51 Main Street, Knysna. Tel: 0445–22127. Breakfast, lunch and dinner daily. Booking recommended.

GRAHAMSTOWN
The Cock House RR
A restored settler home offering breakfast, lunch and dinner daily. Good wine list.
10 Market Street. Tel: 0461–311287.

PORT ELIZABETH
Sir Rufane Donkin Rooms RR
Specialities include the pâté plate (*biltong, brinjal*) and tandoori chicken.
5 George Street. Tel: 041–55 5534. Lunch Monday to Friday, dinner Monday to Saturday.

TULBAGH
Paddagang Wine House RR
Traditional Cape menu includes smoked snoek pâté, Boland trout and *bobotie*, served al fresco on an idyllic terrace.
23 Church Street. Tel: 0236–300242. Open daily, breakfast, tea, lunch, wine-tastings. Booking essential.

WINELANDS
See page 169.

KWAZULU/NATAL

DURBAN
Adega RR
The best of many Portuguese restaurants.
Parry Road. Tel: 031–304 6476. Lunch and dinner Monday to Saturday.
Pakistani RR
Curry is practically the national dish in this section of the country.
80 West Street. Tel: 031–326883. No alcohol allowed. Lunch and dinner Tuesday to Sunday. Booking advisable.
Queen's Tavern R
British Raj-influenced curries, mini stuffed poppadums, prawn curry, samosas, hot chocolate Wellington.
16 Stamford Hill Road, Greyville. Tel: 031–309 4017. Open: daily.
Ulundi R
Colonial-style favourite with Bombay fish curry, lamb *tharkaree* and chefs in turbans.
Royal Hotel, 267 Smith Street. Tel: 031–304 0331. Lunch and dinner Monday to Saturday.

Durban Coffee Shops
Café Jungle Rendezvous
Sherwood Jungle Nursery, Jan Smuts Avenue. Tel: 031–28 2071.
In B'tween
Greenacres Passage, off Smith Street. Tel: 031–301 1704.

Taking refreshment in the cool setting of Johannesburg's Market Theatre Precinct

GAUTENG
JOHANNESBURG
Anton van Wouw RR
Popular with theatregoers, it has a full menu of game, *boboties*, *bredies*, and South African puddings.
111 Sivewright Avenue, Doornfontein. Tel: 011–402 7916. Closed all day Sunday. Booking advisable.

Carnivore RR
A chance to try crocodile, springbok, ostrich or wildebeest.
Muldersdrift Estates, Plot 69, Muldersdrift. Tel: 011–957 2099. Lunch and dinner daily.

Gramadoelas at the Market RR
Pivotal venue for visitors in search of the New South Africa and its table.
Market Theatre Precinct, corner of Bree and Wolhuter streets. Tel: 011–838 6960. Closed Sunday.

The Hut (La Palhota) R
Authentic Angolan/Portuguese peasant cooking.
59b Troye and Pritchard Street, central Johannesburg. Tel: 011–337 6377. Open daily, booking advisable.

Ile de France RRR
One of the finest establishments in town.
Cramerview Centre, 277 Main Road, Bryanston. Tel: 011–706 2837. Lunch Sunday to Friday. Dinner daily. Booking essential.

La Rochelle Beer Hall R
Portuguese cuisine in family atmosphere.
6th Street, La Rochelle. Tel: 011–435 3809. Booking essential at weekends.

Sam's Café R
Sidewalk restaurant in a picturesque street in a fashionable suburb. Chic and cheerful.
11b 7th Avenue, Mellville. Tel: 011–726 8142.

Johannesburg Coffee Shops
Café Camara
Killarney Mall, Riviera Road, Killarney. Tel: 011–486 0235.

DJ's Dressings
The Firs, Rosebank. Tel: 011–880 9711.

Gelati Monte Cristallo
The Mews, Oxford Road, Rosebank. Tel: 011–442 6942.

Park Café
Hyde Park Shopping Centre, Hyde Park.
Tel: 011–880 1231.

PRETORIA
Gerhardt Moerdyk RRR
The food is what South Africa does best:
mealie bread, springbok pie, ostrich, local
fish like snoek and kabeljou ...
752 Park Street, Arcadia, Pretoria. Tel:
012–344 4856. Closed lunchtime Saturday,
all day Sunday. Booking essential.

Die Werf RR
Dine on Cape chicken pie and spicy
mutton *bobotie* or *braai*-ed snoek, 20
minutes from town.
Olympus Drive, Lynnwood. Tel: 012–991
1809. Tuesday to Sunday, breakfast, lunch
and dinner.

Pretoria Coffee Shops
Café de la Dernière Rose
Venning Park, Arcadia. Tel: 012–342
2064.
Coffee Palette
Pretoria Art Museum, Arcadia. Tel:
012–343 7564.
Les Temps des Fondue
91 Gerhardt Moerdyk Street, Sunnyside.
Tel: 012–341 3004.

DRINK
Whether they are drinking bottled Castle
lager on a beach or rum in a *shebeen*
(illegal drinking den), South Africans are
noted hard drinkers. Spirits are relatively
cheap and most international brands are
readily available; locally produced beer
and, more particularly, wine are very
good indeed. South Africans buy their
booze in 'bottle stores'. If offered
'*mampoer*', a clear peach brandy, or
'*witblitz*', a home-made spirit made of just
about anything, then proceed with
caution. These are delicious, potent

WINE ROUTES
The best way to learn about South
African wine is to visit the vineyards of
the Cape. Follow one of the many
routes across the winelands –
hundreds of kilometres of mountains
and valleys – through a series of
official wine-making districts with
considerable climatic differences.
There, sometimes for a tiny fee, it is
possible to taste the full range of estate
produce, buy it or organise its export
home. Many estates, like Boschendal,
Groot Constantia and Vergelegen, also
have historic houses; others have or
are close to restaurants.
   Further information (maps, routes,
opening times and so on) from
Captour (tel: 021–418 5214).
Vineyard Ventures (tel: 021–434
8888) organise tours to selected
estates for serious wine-tasters. John
Platter's *South African Wine Guide*,
(published and updated annually by
John and Erica Platter), is available at
all wine route destinations and good
bookshops.

home-brews with very high levels of
alcohol.

Beer
Beer is the national drink. No social
occasion is complete without it. The local
varieties – Castle, Lion, Ohlssons and
Hansa – are well worth trying, but
international varieties are available.
Indigenous African beer is called *maheu*.
Made from sorghum, it is sour, thick and
hard to stomach at first.

Wine
See pages 170–1.

In world terms, the South African wine industry is small, accounting for about 3.3 per cent of the entire international output. Since sanctions were lifted, South African wine exports to Britain have overtaken those from Chile and New Zealand, and are creeping up fast behind Australian.

The best-known grapes grown locally are, among the whites, Steen (Chenin Blanc), Riesling (both the local Cape Riesling and the unrelated European Weisser Riesling), Chardonnay, Colombar, Muscat d'Alexandrie (Hanepoot – used mainly to produce sweet dessert wines), Palomino, Green Cape and Bukettraube. Among the reds are Cabernet Sauvignon, Cinsaut, Pinotage, Shiraz and Pinot Noir.

Of all the New World wine-producing areas, the Cape has the longest history of viticulture. The first vineyards were planted in 1655, and the first pressing took place in 1659. Stellenbosch's Rustenberg estate has been producing wine for 300 years, while the Klein Constantia vineyards (recently restored) grew some of the earliest wines in the Cape in the 17th century. Meerlust, an historic estate between Cape Town

VINEYARDS

With the lifting of trade sanctions, South Africa is recovering its early reputation as a producer of quality wines

and Stellenbosch has been in the Myburgh family for seven generations; as in Italy, France, Portugal and Spain, the threads of family tradition are hard to break.

Sweet Muscat from Constantia, from vineyards first planted in the 1680s with help from the French Huguenots, made tolerable Napoleon's St Helena exile, while Jane Austen recommended that a heroine try it 'for its healing powers on a disappointed heart'.

Some of South Africa's best wines come from Klein Constantia (Sauvignon Blanc) on Cape Town's outskirts, Meerlust (Pinot Noir and the Bordeaux-style Rubicon) near Stellenbosch, and from the Hamilton Russell Vineyards (Pinot Noir and Chardonnay) at Hermanus. But many other estates produce excellent wines, among them Boschendal (Pinot Noir and Sauvignon Blanc), Backsberg (Pinotage and Chardonnay), Villiera (Merlot) and L'Ormarins (Shiraz).

Hotels and Accommodation

*A*ccommodation ranges from excellent-quality luxury hotels to bed and breakfast establishments and tented encampments in the wilds. Not everybody wants to stay in a hotel. By their very nature hotels cocoon their guests from the realities of life in the host state. Some visitors might like to get closer to nature, or gain a better understanding of the locals. Others want total privacy and the chance to cater for themselves. The alternatives to hotels are growing rapidly. Ideas are even being mooted to provide 'township accommodation': stay *en famille* in a shanty. However, until safety and security are improved, this is an ill-advised choice.

HOTELS
Grading and classification
The South African Tourism Board (SATOUR) has introduced a voluntary system of grading and classification. Hotels applying to join (many excellent ones do not) are graded on a star basis – standard one-star to luxury five-star. A

National Accessibility Programme, also voluntary, indicates the extent and range of facilities offered by member establishments for the disabled tourist.

Luxury or outstanding
Whether they belong to SATOUR's scheme or not, there are some excellent top of the range places to stay in South Africa. In Cape Town, the **Mount Nelson** and **The Bay Hotel** indicate

Many private game lodges provide excellent accommodation, like this one at Sabi Sand

Good for families: the Royal Natal National Park Hotel in the Drakensberg

two opposing poles of style: one is traditional and sedate, the other glamorous and slick. Here, too, among the best, are **The Hohenort Country House Hotel**, **The Vineyard** and **The Alphen**. Out in the Western Cape, Stellenbosch's Cape Dutch **Lanzerac** and Plettenberg Bay's **Plettenberg Park** are unbeatable. In Johannesburg, the best are **The Carlton Hotel** and the **Sandton Sun** and, not far away, **Sun City** and **The Lost City** are extravaganzas of escapism Las Vegas style (see page 74). In Durban the **Royal Hotel** is excellent and, in the Northern Transvaal, so too is Tzaneen's **Coach House Hotel**. Many private game lodges fit this category, including, in KwaZulu/Natal, **Phinda Resource Reserve's Forest Lodge** and **Singita in the Sabi Sand Game Reserve**, on the edge of the Kruger National Park.

Excellent or very good

In SATOUR's rating, these are the three- or two-star establishments which offer good value and comfortable accommodation. Many of the best are listed in the *Portfolio Collection of Country Places* (see box on page 174). There are country houses and lodges, some in Mediterranean style, others reflecting a bush setting. Many chain and business hotels fall into this category.

Comfortable and standard

Generally inexpensive, this category is by far the biggest in SATOUR's rating classification. Many are owner run, and there are few frills attached, but this is not necessarily an indication of low standards. These are places which provide adequate accommodation, good choices if you intend to be out all day.

Budget

There is a paucity of accommodation in this field. Youth hostels, camp sites and caravan parks generally provide the best of what is available in this category. Youth hostel membership is preferred but not essential. See **Student and Youth Travel**, page 187.

Bed and breakfasts and guesthouses

South Africans generally have an excellent sense of hospitality, which is put to good use on guests staying in one of the many B and Bs dotted around the country. There are literally hundreds of these in private homes. Many are situated in areas which lack hotels, others proliferate in tourist areas. While you breakfast in the company of the host or hostess, some have private entrances and all have private bathrooms. Some are self-catering accommodation in detached cottages.

THOMAS COOK
Traveller's Tip

Travellers who purchase their travel tickets from a Thomas Cook network location are entitled to use the services of any other Thomas Cook Network location, free of charge, to make hotel reservations.

THE ALTERNATIVES

Caravanning

South Africa is filled with caravan sites, this being one of the most popular forms of weekend or holiday recreation. The National Parks Board and the Natal Parks Board (see **National Parks**, page 185) both have a range of beautiful sites in their reserves and resorts. Many are equipped with tennis courts, open-air cooking facilities and ablutions blocks and are located near places to swim.

Health spas

Most health spas and hydros are based on hot mineral springs. Facilities vary: up-market ones offer the ultimate in self-indulgent pampering, recuperation therapy, nutrition and lifestyle education programmes or private nursing. Some have tennis courts, gyms, hiking or mountain bike trails. Most have swimming pools. Accommodation ranges from luxury to self catering chalets or flats. Find out about spas from SATOUR.

Private reserves and ranches

Private game reserves offer a wide range of highly characterful accommodation. At the upper end of the scale, they are superb, and with limited numbers, guests get personal attention from game rangers – a definite advantage. A secondary category offers 'prestige' ranches, often family run and again with highly personal service. **Portfolio** (see box opposite) looks after a number of these.
Prices from around R185 per person per night sharing.

Rented accommodation

This is rapidly becoming a popular alternative. Accommodation varies considerably, ranging from top-grade

Oceanside camp and caravan site. Caravanning is a popular South African pastime

Rough it in style at the Meerhof Lodge in the Cedarberg Mountains

private houses with pools and a view to converted servants' quarters lacking privacy, or poky holiday flats in apartment blocks. Many are highly desirable, others are dreadful. Some are in holiday complexes with shared pools, others are located in suburbs or at the sea. Before you pay your deposit make sure that the booking agency has been vetted by the local tourist office. Prices increase over the December and January period, particularly in Cape Town and the coastal areas of the Western Cape.
Prices from around R70 per person per night.

Staying on a farm
Country wide, farmers are opening their homes and enterprises to paying guests looking for a genuine introduction to the countryside. Farms vary from small intensive operations to large ranches; some are situated close to game reserves and hunting lodges, providing the additional advantage of game-spotting. There is a range of options from self-catering to bed and breakfast, or full board. Accommodation might be in a thatched *rondawel* or cottage, in an annexe to the farmhouse or in the farmhouse itself. Privacy is virtually guaranteed because scope for a large number of guests is limited. Most often food is good country cooking. Fishing, walking, birdwatching, mountain climbing, swimming or tennis are some of the activities available.
Prices from R70.00 (self catering with maid service).

On Business

Sanctions and disinvestment brought South Africa to its knees. Out in the cold, economic growth was imperceptible, but today South Africa is back into global investment, tourism and trade markets, with new rules being developed to guide the way its people do business both locally and internationally.

South Africa has the capacity to become one of the world's leading points of growth. In answer to criticisms that high crime rates, huge unemployment, poverty, spiralling wage costs, uncertain tax laws and political and economic instability are putting investors off, the Government of National Unity has stated that it is committed to improving and safeguarding foreign investment, citing lowered corporate tax and plans to improve education and general skill levels. It also remains committed to the promotion of regional political and economic stability.

All of this is only possible with high and sustainable growth. To this end, the Reconstruction and Development Programme (RDP) seeks to mobilise the whole population and the country's resources toward the final eradication of the results of apartheid and the building of a democratic, non-racial and non-sexist future. It aims at the creation of a prosperous society on a sustainable and environmentally friendly path of growth and development. If the RDP can be translated into an actual government programme, South African society will be like no other – and business opportunities will be endless.

BUSINESS HOURS
Most offices are open 8am–5pm, weekdays. People take an hour for lunch between noon and 2pm, and some do limited hours on Saturday mornings.

BUSINESS ETIQUETTE
People are usually efficient, courteous and punctual in South Africa. You should be the same. Take plenty of business cards and dole them out liberally. In black culture, lay your left hand lightly on your right wrist when shaking hands and give and take anything, however small, with both hands as a mark of respect. The local club and/or golf course are crucial business venues, while societies such as Rotary, Lions and Round Table are of far greater importance than in Europe. South Africa is enormously hospitable and hard-drinking. Expect to be invited home, and arm yourself with some small gifts accordingly.

BUSINESS MEDIA
There are regular business reports on TV and radio and in all the major newspapers. There is also a dedicated paper, the *Business Daily*. For international business, BBC World Service, CNN and Sky news all have business reports and CNN teletext offers up-to-the-minute briefings. International papers and magazines such as *Time* and *Newsweek* are on sale in major cities within two to three days of publication.

BUSINESS SERVICES
All major city hotels have some secretarial services. The local Yellow Pages will be able to offer others, and you will find interpreters in Cape Town, Jo'burg and Durban. English is the main language of

Mercury holding a bag of gold symbolises commerce in Pretoria

business and government. Vodacom have 24-hour desks at all major international airports offering hire of mobile phones.

CONFERENCES

Many of the larger hotels and even relatively small game lodges offer some conference facilities. What is lacking at present is a home for major international events. However, both Cape Town and Durban are currently planning massive new conference centres.

Durban

The **Durban Convention & Conference Bureau** has been set up to assist those arranging conferences, conventions, product launches or special events. Its extensive data bank contains detailed information on venues, guest speakers, entertainers, etc. It is a free consultancy service. The Bureau publishes a booklet on pre- and post-conference tours, and the *Greater Durban Marketing Authority Convention* booklet outlining the services on offer. *PO Box 1044 Durban 4000. Tel: 031/3044934.*

Johannesburg

Of South Africa's urban population, 43 per cent live in Johannesburg. It generates more than 40 per cent of the country's gross domestic product and 60 per cent of its manufacturing output, and boasts an abundance of professional and managerial talent, a close proximity to financial markets, energy sources and transportation networks, and a sound commercial and financial infrastructure. As well as an enormous range of hotel accommodation, Johannesburg has 34 well appointed conference and exhibition venues, the largest being NASREC, which can accommodate up to 5,000 people in seven rooms.

FURTHER INFORMATION

American Chamber of Commerce in South Africa
Tel: 011–880 163.
Department of Home Affairs (immigration and work permits)
Tel: 012–314 8911.
Department of Manpower
Tel: 012–310 6911.
Industrial Development and Investment Centre (IDIC)
Tel: 012–310 9786.
Johannesburg Chamber of Commerce:
Information Desk: Tel: 011–726 5300.
Industrial Relations Hotline: Tel: 011–643 6762.
Trade Department: Tel: 011–726 5300.
Johannesburg Stock Exchange
Tel: 011–833 6580.
SATOUR
Conference Promotion Division (tel: 012–347 0600), or branches in foreign capitals.
Small Business Development and Small Business Centre Corporation
Tel: 011–643 7351.
South Africa Chamber of Business
Tel: 011–482 2524.
South African British Trade Association (SABRITA)
Tel: 011–838 4784.

Practical Guide

CONTENTS

ARRIVING

Documents

Visitors must hold a valid passport, endorsed with a visa if required (holders of passports from Australia, Canada, Ireland, New Zealand, United Kingdom and the United States do not need a visa). UK subjects require a full British passport, valid for at least six months beyond the intended stay.

For information on passport and visa requirements, contact your local passport office or the diplomatic or consular representative of the South African Government. Proof is required that you can support yourself in South Africa. If you do not have a return ticket, you must show that you have the means to buy one.

By air

International airports at Johannesburg, Cape Town and Durban have regular scheduled flights from all over the world. South African Airways (SAA) is the state airline.

AIRPORT TAX

R20 arrival tax is included in the price of an international ticket, R5 in the cost of a domestic ticket. A tax of R40 is collected on arrival at Skukuza (Kruger National Park) airport if visiting a private game reserve, less if staying in the Kruger.

Airline offices include:
South African Airways (SAA)
PO Box 7778, Johannesburg 2000.
Tel: 011–333 6504.
Air France
PO Box 41022, 2024 Craighall.
Tel: 011–880 8055.
Alitalia
PO Box 937, 2116 Northlands.
Tel: 011–880 9259.

British Airways
PO Box 535, 2121 Parklands.
Tel: 011–441 8600.
KLM Royal Dutch Airlines
PO Box 8624, 2000 Johannesburg.
Tel: 011–881 9696.
Lufthansa
PO Box 1083, 2000 Johannesburg.
Tel: 011–484 4711.
Qantas
PO Box 651350, 2010 Benmore.
Tel: 011–884 5300.
For other airlines, see the phone book.

The main airports are:
Johannesburg International (25km east of Johannesburg). Serving both Johannesburg and Pretoria,this is an international terminus with extensive duty free facilities. Scheduled bus services are available between airport and city centres, taxis are readily to hand, and larger car rental companies are represented.
General enquiries: Tel: 011–975 9963.
Cape Town Airport. A scheduled, half-hourly bus service connects airport and city centre (about 20km). Taxis are available and all the major car hire companies are represented.
Flight details: Tel: 021–934 0444.
Durban Airport. A regular bus service connects airport and city centre (about 20km). Taxis are available and all major car hire companies are represented.
Flight details: Tel: 031–426 156.

By land
South Africa has land borders with Namibia, Botswana, Zimbabwe, Mozambique, Swaziland and Lesotho. All are open at the time of writing.
   The Thomas Cook Overseas Timetable, published bi-monthly, gives details of many rail, bus and shipping services worldwide, and is a help when planning a rail journey to, from and around South Africa. Available in the UK from some stations, any branch of Thomas Cook, or by phoning 01733–268943; in the USA from Forsyth Travel Library Inc, 9154 West 57th Street (PO Box 2975), Shawness Mission, Kansas 66201 (tel: 800–367 7982, toll-free – from within US only).

By sea
A number of shipping companies provide cargo/passenger services linking South Africa and Europe. CTC Cruise Lines, P&O Cruises, Royal Viking Line and Starlauro are known to be planning cruises calling at South African ports.

Permitted imports
Currency Only R500 in South African Reserve Bank notes can be imported, while unlimited foreign currency and travellers' cheques are allowed, provided they are declared on arrival. Foreign passport holders may not take out more foreign currency than they declared on arrival.
Drugs Narcotics and habit-forming drugs are prohibited.
Duty-free allowance 400 cigarettes, 250 grammes of tobacco and 50 cigars, one litre of spirit, two litres of wine, 50ml of perfume and 250ml of toilet water.

Conversion Table

FROM	TO	MULTIPLY BY
Inches	Centimetres	2.54
Feet	Metres	0.3048
Yards	Metres	0.9144
Miles	Kilometres	1.6090
Acres	Hectares	0.4047
Gallons	Litres	4.5460
Ounces	Grams	28.35
Pounds	Grams	453.6
Pounds	Kilograms	0.4536
Tons	Tonnes	1.0160

To convert back, for example from centimetres to inches, divide by the number in the the third column.

Men's Suits

UK		36	38	40	42	44	46	48
Rest of Europe	46	48	50	52	54	56	58
US		36	38	40	42	44	46	48

Dress Sizes

UK		8	10	12	14	16	18
France		36	38	40	42	44	46
Italy		38	40	42	44	46	48
Rest of Europe		34	36	38	40	42	44
US		6	8	10	12	14	16

Men's Shirts

UK	14	14.5	15	15.5	16	16.5	17
Rest of Europe	36	37	38 39/40	41	42 43
US	14	14.5	15	15.5	16	16.5	17

Men's Shoes

UK	7	7.5 8.5	9.5	10.5	11
Rest of Europe	41	42 43	44	45 46
US	8	8.5 9.5	10.5	11.5	12

Women's Shoes

UK	4.5	5 5.5	6	6.5	7
Rest of Europe	38	38	39	39	40	41
US	6 6.5	7	7.5	8 8.5

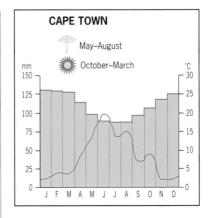

CAPE TOWN

☂ May–August
☀ October–March

CAMPING AND CARAVANNING

Both camping and caravanning are exceptionally good value. Sites are inexpensive, generally well located and, although basic, they are well cared for and accessible. Information about them is provided by the local tourist body.

CHILDREN

See pages 152–3.

CLIMATE

See charts.

CONVERSION TABLES

See tables opposite.

CRIME

See page 32.

DRIVING

Car rental

Car rental is expensive. Major international companies are represented throughout and offer a range of vehicles from economy-class to the latest quality models. Smaller local firms have slightly lower prices but charge a fee per kilometre – advantageous for limited city

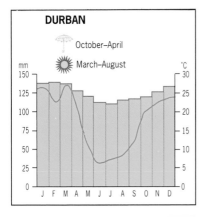

DURBAN

October–April

March–August

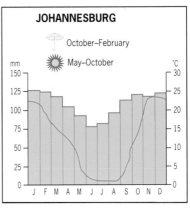

JOHANNESBURG

October–February

May–October

WEATHER CONVERSION CHART
25.4mm = 1 inch
°F = 1.8 × °C + 32

driving but expensive for long-distance travel. Look for special deals which offer free daily mileage. You need a valid driver's licence and usually a minimum age (23 or 25) is specified.

Avis
PO Box 221, Isando 1600. Tel: 0800 021111 (tollfree) or 021–934 0216.
Budget
PO Box 1777 Kempton Park 1620. Tel: 0800 016622 (tollfree) or 011–392 3907.
Dolphin
PO Box 4613, Kempton Park 1620. Tel: 0800 011344 (tollfree).
Imperial
PO Box 260177 Excom 2023. Tel: 0800 131000 (tollfree) or 011–337 2300.
Note: tollfree numbers can only be called from within South Africa.

On the road
South Africa has one of the worst driving records in the world, so be vigilant. An excellent road network exists, and you drive on the left. The speed limit in built-up areas is 60kph, on rural roads 100kph and on freeways 120kph unless otherwise indicated. Traffic laws are strictly enforced: seat belts are compulsory; carry your driving licence; do not drive under the influence of alcohol. A valid driver's licence, provided that it is in English and that a photograph is an integral part of the licence, is accepted. Otherwise obtain an International Driving Permit before departure.

Filling stations are plentiful on major routes, infrequent on others. Some open 24 hours a day, most are open 7am–7pm. Long-distance travellers should take spare petrol. Pay for fuel with cash – credit cards are not accepted

(some banks issue special 'petrocards'). Some roads have small tolls depending on the route and type of vehicle, so carry a little cash.

For expert advice contact the Automobile Association of South Africa, tel: 0800 010101 (tollfree). Head office: AA House, 66 De Korte Street, Braamfontein 2001 (tel: 011–407 1000).

ELECTRICITY

Urban power systems are generally 220/230 volts AC (250 in Pretoria). Adaptors for shavers and driers are available locally.

EMBASSIES AND CONSULATES

South African embassies world wide:
Australia
Rhodes Place, State Circle, Yarralumla, Canberra, ACT 2600. Tel: 62–273 2424.
Canada
15 Sussex Drive, Ottawa, Ontario K1M 1M8. Tel: 613–744 0330.
Ireland
See the United Kingdom office.
United Kingdom
Trafalgar Square, London, WC2N 5DP. Tel: 0171–930 4488.
United States
3051 Massachusetts Avenue, NW, Washington DC 20008. Tel: 202–232 4400.

Foreign embassies in South Africa:
Australia
292 Orient Street, Arcadia, Pretoria. Tel: 012–325 4315.
Canada
1103 Arcadia Street, Hatfield, Pretoria. Tel: 012–324 6923.
Ireland
Tulbagh Park, 1234 Church Street, Colbyn, Pretoria. Tel: 012–342 5062.
United Kingdom

'Greystoke' 225 Hill Street, Arcadia, Pretoria. Tel: 012–43 3121.
United States
877 Pretorius Street, Arcadia, Pretoria. Tel: 012–342 1048.

EMERGENCIES

Police emergency: Tel: 10111.
Police Crime Stop: Tel: 0800 11 12 13.
Ambulance, Fire, Mountain Rescue, Poisoning, Air and Sea Rescue: Tel: 1022 and ask for the relevant service.

The Thomas Cook Worldwide Customer Promise offers free emergency assistance at any Thomas Cook Network location to travellers who have purchased their travel tickets at a Thomas Cook Network location. In addition, any MasterCard cardholder may use any Thomas Cook Network location to report loss or theft of their card and obtain an emergency card replacement, as a free service under the Thomas Cook MasterCard International Alliance.

Thomas Cook MasterCard Refund Centre (24-hour service – report loss or theft within 24 hours): +44 1733 318950.

GAY AND LESBIAN

Gay and Lesbian Counselling Service, PO Box 785493, Sandton 2146, Johannesburg, tel: 011–643 2311, can be contacted daily 7pm–10pm and will put you in touch with other, equivalent services around the country. They do not supply information about gay and lesbian venues such as clubs.

GETTING AROUND
By air

South African Airways operates a domestic service between Johannesburg and major centres, and between other, smaller centres. It also offers a range of special deals for overseas travellers.

Regional carriers offer services to smaller destinations, supplemented by several charter and safari-flight operators. If you have a private light aircraft licence, bring it. Rates for the rental of light aircraft are affordable for international visitors.

By rail

There is an efficient long-distance service connecting major cities. Some routes involve overnight travel; services include sleeping berths, private compartments, and a dining car. First- and second-class tickets must be booked at least 24 hours in advance: Cape Town, tel: 021–218 3871; Durban, tel: 031–302 2921; Johannesburg, tel: 011–773 2944. Most stations accept bookings. Ask about discounts for first-class travel. See also pages 136–7.

By bus and express coach

A large number of daily coach services operate on inter-city routes, day or night. Always book your ticket 24 hours in advance.

Greyhound – information, tel: 011–333 2139, reservations, tel: 011–333 2130.
Translux Express – reservations and enquiries, tel: 011–774 3333 or 3871.
Intercape – reservations and enquiries, tel: 011–333 5231 or 021–934 4400.

By car

See **Driving**, page 180.

Hitch-hiking

Although hitch-hiking is widespread, as many South Africans do not own cars, it is inadvisable for tourists. Be cautious before giving lifts. Organise lifts through noticeboards at Backpackers in Cape Town (tel: 021–234 530) or noticeboards at the tourist information offices in other cities.

The famous and luxurious Blue Train snakes its way through the mountains

Public transport in cities

See page 187.

HEALTH

AIDS

As everywhere, be cautious about HIV infection and take the usual precautions. AIDS is highly prevalent (and on the increase) in African countries, and South Africa is no exception. Unlike Europe, it is on the increase in Africa.

Drinking water

Tap water is purified and is 100 per cent safe to drink.

Hospitals and doctors

Doctors are listed in local telephone directories under 'Medical Practitioners'.

Inoculations

No vaccination certificates are required by visitors from the UK, but inoculation against TB, typhoid and tetanus is advisable.

Malaria and bilharzia precautions

Visitors to Mpumalanga (Eastern

Transvaal) lowveld, the Kruger National Park and the game reserves of KwaZulu/Natal must take anti-malaria tablets before, during and after their stay. It is inadvisable to swim in rivers and lakes in the eastern and northern regions of the country as the bilharzia parasite may be present.

Sunburn

Skin cancer is the most common cancer among South African whites. Avoid the most intense hours of sunlight – 11am–3pm – and remember that water provides little protection against ultraviolet (UV) radiation; the skin is still bombarded by UV rays on a cloudy day, and UV penetrates fabric. Light coloured clothing can filter out the sun and reflect the heat, keeping you cool. Always wear a hat. Sun protection measures are vital for young children. Dress them in loose protective clothing and make sure they wear hats with a brim. Use sunscreen with at least a SPF 15+. For more information on skin cancer, and the rules of sunbathing, call the **Cancer Association of South Africa** (CANSA), tel: 0800 226622.

INSURANCE

South Africa has no national health scheme. Medical treatment must be paid for by the patient, so take out travel insurance which covers accidents, illness or hospitalisation. Travel insurance policies can be purchased through the AA, branches of Thomas Cook, and most travel agents. For drivers, Third Party Insurance is built into the price of fuel.

MAPS

Excellent regional and city maps are available from SATOUR and individual local publicity associations (see **Tourist Offices**, page 189). Nationwide, CNA booksellers have a good range of local guides and maps.

MEDIA

The South African Broadcasting Corporation broadcasts 22 radio services in 11 languages, and four television services in seven languages. Programmes include news, actuality, interviews, sport, documentaries and films. The M-Net TV cable network, an independent subscription service, broadcasts mainly in English, and concentrates on entertainment. More than 5,000 periodicals, journals, newspapers and magazines are published on a regular basis. Five daily national and five Sunday national newspapers are published. Of the daily papers, the *Sowetan* has the highest circulation, followed by *The Star* and then the *Sunday Times*. Read the *Weekly Mail & Guardian* for international news and comment.

MONEY MATTERS

Currency

The South African currency unit is the Rand, denoted by the symbol R (international symbol ZAR). It is divided into 100 cents (c). Bank notes are issued in denominations of R200, R100, R50, R20 and R10 (R5 are being phased out). Coins come in 1, 2, 5 (being phased out), 10, 20, and 50c; R1 and R2.

Exchange facilities

Identification is required by all banks when changing money. Shop around for cheaper commission rates, otherwise the standard is R10 per transaction.

Credit cards

Most businesses, tour operators, airlines, hotels and restaurants accept international credit cards including VISA, MasterCard, American Express and Diners Club. Petrol stations don't accept them (see page 181).

Thomas Cook

Thomas Cook MasterCard and travellers' cheques free you from the hazards of carrying large amounts of cash, and in the event of loss or theft, can quickly be refunded. US dollar cheques are recommended, though cheques in all other currencies are acceptable. Hotels, shops and restaurants in tourist and urban areas will accept travellers' cheques in lieu of cash.

NATIONAL HOLIDAYS

1 January New Year's Day
21 March Human Rights Day
Variable Good Friday
Variable Easter Monday
27 April Freedom Day
1 May Workers' Day
16 June Youth Day
9 August National Women's Day
24 September Heritage Day
16 December Day of Reconciliation
25 December Christmas Day/Goodwill Day.

OPENING HOURS

Banks are open 9am–3.30pm, Monday to Friday, and 8.30am–11am on Saturdays. Automatic Teller Machines (ATMs) are situated outside most banks and are open 24 hours a day.
Shops are open 8am–5pm, Monday to Friday, and 8.30am–1.00pm on Saturdays – although in the main shopping areas hours are generally extended. Bottle stores open 9am–6pm Monday to Saturday.
See also **Post**, page 186.

PARKS AND RESERVES

National Parks

Country wide, these are run by the National Parks Board, except in KwaZulu/Natal where they are the responsibility of the Natal Parks Board. Most provide a range of rest camp accommodation, have at least one restaurant, a provisions store and fuel. Some have their own post office, fax facilities and laundry facilities. Entrances to parks and reserves usually close at sunset: aim to arrive well before that. Preference is given to written applications received 13 months in advance. Before booking, check that the park of your choice contains the animals you want to see.
National Parks Board, PO Box 787 Pretoria 0001, tel: 012–343 1991.
National Parks Board Hotline, tel: 012–343 2006, fax: 012–343 2007 for foreign visitors.
Natal Parks Board, PO Box 662, Pietermaritzburg 3200, tel: 0331–47 1981.

Private reserves

These tend to market themselves through their rest camps, some of which provide

---

AFRIKAANS/XHOSA PHRASES

yes *ja* (Afrikaans), *ewe* (Xhosa)
no *nee* (Afrikaans), *hayi* (Xhosa)
how are you? *hoe gaan dit?* (Afrikaans), *kunjani?* (Xhosa)
thank you *dankie* (Afrikaans), *enkosi* (Xhosa)
how much? *hoeveel?* (Afrikaans), *yimalini?* (Xhosa)
good morning *goeimôre* (Afrikaans), *molo* (Xhosa)
where is the post office/bank/hotel? *waar is die poskantoor/bank/hotel?* (Afrikaans), *iphi iposi/ibhanki/ ihotele?* (Xhosa)

accommodation among South Africa's most luxurious (see page 174).

Other parks and reserves

Many parks and reserves fall under the auspices of local conservation bodies. These are noted for their scenic beauty rather than their abundance of game. They offer walking, hiking and climbing. For further information, contact regional offices:

Cape Nature Conservation, PO Box X9086, Cape Town, tel: 021–483 4085.
Department of Nature Conservation, PO Box 517, Bloemfontein, Free State, tel: 051–70511.
Transvaal Nature Conservation, Private Bag X209, Pretoria 0001, tel: 012–201 4358.

PHARMACIES
Cape Town

K's Pharmacy, 52 Regent Road, Sea Point, tel: 021–434 9331. Open: 9am–9pm.
Rustenberg Pharmacy, Rondebosch Shopping Centre, Main Road, Rondebosch, tel: 021–685 5998. Open: 8.30am–10pm.

Durban

No 24-hour pharmacies, but **Medical Chest Chemist**, 155 Berea Road, Berea, tel: 031–305 6151, and **Day & Night Chemist**, 9a Nedband Circle, corner of Point Road and West Street, tel: 031–368 3666 are open late.

Johannesburg

Express Pharmacy, 42 Wolmaran Street, Joubert Park, tel: 011–729 2222.

PLACES OF WORSHIP

Churches of every denomination, synagogues, mosques and Hindu temples are all represented in abundance. Generally, South Africa's population is religiously oriented and religious beliefs play an important role in public affairs.

POLICE

The South African Police (SAP) can be contacted 24 hours a day. See listings as SA Police Service under Government Departments in local phone directories.

POST

Post office hours are 8.30am–4.30pm, Monday, Tuesday, Thursday and Friday; 9am–4.30pm, Wednesday; 8am–noon, Saturday (smaller offices close for lunch 1–2pm).

Identification is required when using the *poste restante* service offered by the General Post Offices. Hours: 8am–4.30pm Monday to Friday, and 8am–noon on Saturday.

Main post offices:
Cape Town: GPO, corner of Parliament and Darling streets, tel: 021–409 9111.
Durban: GPO, corner of West and Gardiner streets, tel: 031–305 7521.
Johannesburg: GPO, Jeppe Street, between Von Brandis and the Mall, tel: 011–222 9111.

PRICES AND TAX

South Africa is no longer a 'cheap' destination'. People generally expect to pay less because they are going to Africa. Having said that, petrol is inexpensive, as are local wines, spirits and tobacco. Hotel prices are slightly lower than their European or American equivalents.

VAT at the rate of 14 per cent is levied on most items and services, including hotel accommodation, goods, transport and tours. VAT can be claimed back on goods purchased at a price exceeding R250 at the international departure point.

PUBLIC TRANSPORT

Public transport in South Africa is erratic and unsafe.

Buses

Durban has a more efficient bus service than either Cape Town or Johannesburg. This, the Mynah Shuttle Service (tel: 031–307 3503) operates between the city centre and the surrounding suburbs. Durban Transport's blue buses operate in all areas and surrounding suburbs (tel: 031–307 3503). The bus service in Cape Town, as in Johannesburg, is slow and infrequent. Use it during the day if you must, but always take taxis after dark.

Rail

Of the three cities, only Cape Town has an efficient suburban and city rail service. Much used by commuters, it is best avoided after dark.

Taxis

Most cities have minibus taxis which have an extensive and comprehensive service operating day and night. They are inexpensive, but the driving is atrocious, and travel time varies from driver to driver. At night, before getting in, make sure you know where they are going, and remember that townships are not safe. They won't depart until they are full – generally the maximum is 22 people, though often even that is dangerously exceeded. These taxis are also the main form of rural transport. Metered taxi cabs are common but more expensive – though the driving is safer and the service more reliable. They cannot be hailed, you must telephone (look in the Yellow Pages). Some cities – Cape Town and Durban, for example – have *tuk-tuks* or *rikkis*, small open vehicles which will, on request, pick you up or drop you at your door.

SENIOR CITIZENS

Facilities for senior citizens are not comprehensive. In general, expect discounts on cinema and theatre tickets, and there is, with proof of age, occasionally a 5–10 per cent discount on cash purchases in shops, markets and on restaurant bills. This is discretionary so ask for it. There are no discounts on local bus or train travel, though South African Airways offers, with advanced booking, reduced fares (for everybody) on internal flights – 50 per cent reduction if booked a month in advance, and 30 per cent for two-week advance booking. Certain national parks offer discounts on accommodation tariffs. **The Association for Retired Persons and Pensioners** (ARP&P), tel: 021–531 1758.
South African National Council for the Aged, tel: 021–246 270.

STUDENT AND YOUTH TRAVEL

For Student Cards, Youth Discount Cards, Youth Hostel Membership Cards, Medical Travel Insurance, and Student Charter and Standby Fares, contact the **South African Student Travel Service** (SASTS), University of the Witwatersrand, Student Union Building, Ground Floor, East Campus, tel: 011–716 3045. It has offices countrywide. **Hostelling International South Africa** (HISA), 101 Boston House, 46 Strand Street, Cape Town 8001, tel: 021–419 1853, provides a similar service. It also has specific information for backpackers and is a specialist in budget travel.

TELEPHONES

Hotels add a surcharge to your calls. Public call boxes are available for which phonecards can be purchased in pubs, newsagents and so on. Telephone kiosks operate on a minimum of 20c.

The international dialling code for South Africa is 27.

The dialling codes for the main cities within South Africa are:

Cape Town – 021
Durban – 031
Johannesburg – 011
Pretoria – 012

Useful numbers

Directory enquiries: 1023
Telkom information: 0800 12255
International Operator (for booking or placing international calls): 0900
International Directory Enquiries: 0903
Calling collect: Australia 0800 99 0061; Canada 0800 99 0014; UK 0800 9900 44; USA (AT&T) 0800 990 123.

Telex and fax

Most businesses and hotels have fax and telex facilities. Local stationers or 'copy shops' often have faxing facilities. Fax numbers are generally listed in the phone books.

TIME

South African Standard Time throughout the year is two hours ahead of Greenwich Mean Time (Universal Standard Time), one hour ahead of Central European Winter Time, seven hours ahead of US Eastern Standard Winter Time and eight hours behind Australian Eastern Standard Time.

TIPPING

A 10 per cent service charge is generally expected in restaurants, not usually included with the bill. Leave something for hotel staff such as porters and chambermaids. Taxi drivers should receive 10 per cent of the fare on top, and luggage porters R1 per bag.

TOILETS

Most tourist venues, service stations and shopping centres are fairly well served by public lavatories. In nature reserves, parks and at the seaside they may be rather primitive though standards of cleanliness are fairly high. Occasionally users may be charged a small fee.

TOUR OPERATORS AND AGENTS

To obtain a comprehensive list of tour operators in South Africa, contact SATOUR. For specialist safari operators, see **Getting Away From It All**, pages 138–9.

City Tours
Springbok Atlas

Tours of most major cities, daytrips and safaris.
PO Box 819, Cape Town 8000. Tel: 021–448 6545 or fax: 021–47 3835.

Tailor-made tours
African Options

PO Box 9395 Johannesburg 2000. Tel: 011–407 3211.

South African Airways Holidays

All major South African holiday destinations.
Sussex House, London Road, East Grinstead, West Sussex RH19 1LD, UK. Tel: 01342–322525.

18-35s
African Routes

Safaris, hikes, balloon safaris, rafting, diving, adventure trails, houseboats and trans-Africa routes.

PO Box 201700, Durban North 4016.
Tel: 031–833348.

Off-the-beaten-track tours
Epic Expeditions
SA Adventure Centre, 48a Strand Street,
Cape Town. Tel: 021–419 1721.

Children and education
The Wilderness Trust of South
Africa
Young people of 9 to 18 years are taught,
under expert guidance, about the natural
environment.
Box 577 Bedfordview 2008. Tel: 011–531
814.
The National Envir Adventure Trust
The Trust organises adventure camps for
children aged from seven years, with or
without their parents.
PO Box 260 Gilletts 3603. Tel: 031–77
3334.

Student and Youth Travel
See page 187.

Other useful addresses
Association of Southern African
Travel Agents (ASATA)
PO Box 5032, 2000 Johannesburg.
Tel: 011–403 2923.
Department of Environmental
Affairs (Environmental Education)
Environmental Affairs Ct, Foretrust
Building, Martin Hammerschlag Way,
Cape Town 8001. Tel: 021–310 3707.

TOURIST OFFICES
South African Tourist Board
(SATOUR)
Australia and New Zealand
Level 6, 285 Clarence Street, Sydney,
NSW 2000. Tel: 02–261 3424.
United Kingdom (also Eire and
Scandinavia)

5/6 Alt Grove, Wimbledon, London,
SW19 4DZ. Tel: 0181–944 8080.
United States
500 Fifth Avenue, 20th Floor, New York
NY 10110 (tel: 212–730 2929); Suite
1524, 9841 Airport Boulevard, Los
Angeles, 90045 (tel: 310–641 8444).

SATOUR in South Africa:
Cape Town, 10th Floor, Golden Acre,
Private Bag X9108, Cape Town 8000.
Tel: 021–21 6274.
Durban, 22 Gardiner Street, PO Box
2516, Durban 4000. Tel: 031–304 7144.
Johannesburg, Suite 4305, Carlton
Centre, PO Box 1094, Johannesburg
2000. Tel: 011–331 5241.

Most areas have a local publicity
association:
Cape Tourism Authority (Captour),
Tourist Information Centre, 3 Adderley
Street, Cape Town. Tel: 021–418 5214.
Durban Unlimited, PO Box 1044,
Durban 4000. Tel: 031–304 4934.
Johannesburg Publicity Association,
Ground Floor, North State Building,
corner of Kruis and Market streets,
Johannesburg. Tel: 011–29 4961.

TRAVELLERS WITH
DISABILITIES
For information about special needs –
tours accommodating wheelchairs,
services, handbooks, and so on:
National Council for the Physically
Disabled in South Africa, tel: 011–726
8040.
Disabled People of South Africa,
tel: 0431–431 579, is the country's only
pressure group for the disabled.
South African National Council for
the Blind, tel: 012–346 1171.
South African National Council for
the Deaf, tel: 011–482 1610.

ACKNOWLEDGEMENTS

The Automobile Association wishes to thank the following photographers and libraries for their assistance in the preparation of this book.
ALLSPORT 157 (M Hewitt), 159 (D Rogers); DURBAN UNLIMITED 151; MARY EVANS PICTURE LIBRARY 125a; GLOBAL SCENES 18a, 22, 52, 66/7, 68, 72a, 72b, 90, 91, 98a, 98b, 111, 140, 156, 160, 171a, 171b, 183; HULTON DEUTSCH COLLECTION LTD 134a, 134b; HUMAN & ROUSSEAU (PTY) LTD 165a, 165b; NATURE PHOTOGRAPHERS LTD 23a (S Bean); PICTURES COLOUR LIBRARY LTD 88, 131; REX FEATURES LTD 14; SOUTH AFRICAN AIRWAYS 179; SOUTH AFRICAN TOURISM 10, 11, 77b; SPECTRUM COLOUR LIBRARY cover, 5, 15, 51b, 66a, 66b, 70, 79, 104, 105, 124b, 124c, 177; ZEFA PICTURES LTD 125b

All remaining pictures are held in the Association's own library (AA PHOTO LIBRARY) and were taken by Paul Kenward with the exception of pages 4, 18b, 21, 36, 115, 119a, 119b, 122 and 123 which were taken by M Birkitt, pages 60, 63 and 95b which were taken by J Howard and page 27 which was taken by E Meacher.

The author would like to thank the many Duncans for their helpful suggestions, Judith Watt, Mandy and Tessa Katz, Madeleine Masson, Carol Mauerberger, Nikki Meiklejohn (Durban Unlimited), Captour, SATOUR and its various regional offices, and Emma Cunningham of South African Airways for arranging flights to and from South Africa.

CONTRIBUTORS
Series adviser: Melissa Shales   **Designer:** Design 23   **Copy editor:** Audrey Horne
Verifier: Jenny Fry   **Indexer:** Marie Lorimer